BLINDERS

THE DESTRUCTIVE, DOWNSTREAM IMPACT
OF CONTRACEPTION, ABORTION, AND IVF

T0155390

BLINDERS

THE DESTRUCTIVE, DOWNSTREAM IMPACT OF CONTRACEPTION, ABORTION, AND IVF

THOMAS W. HILGERS, MD

BEAUFORT BOOKS
NEW YORK, NEW YORK

**REVEALING THE NEGLECTED AMERICAN PUBLIC HEALTH
CRISIS THAT HAS GROWN TO GIGANTIC PROPORTIONS**

**Library of Congress
Cataloging-in-Publication Data**

Hilgers, Thomas W, 1943–
Thomas W. Hilgers, MD

Includes bibliographical references and index.
ISBN: 978-0-8253-0889-5

**Cover Design: Matthew A. Johnson
Design and Layout: Matthew A. Johnson**

Published by:
Beaufort Books
New York, New York
www.beaufortbooks.com

TABLE OF CONTENTS

INTRODUCTION

Over the last 50 or 60 years, there has appeared a directional shift in the medical and social culture of the United States. We see it in the news programs every night, sometimes several times a night. Often there are generic reasons given for these changes such as "poverty and hopelessness." But could there be other reasons? Could the medical profession be playing an important role in the violence and destructiveness of this cultural shift? Has there been any critical self-examination by the medical profession which usually demands evidence-based conclusions to be assessed? Or are there some questions that are too difficult for individuals to investigate, not because it's impossible to investigate them, but because it can be painful and because the attitudes of a collective group of colleagues may be preventing these questions from being asked. It is as if we have **BLINDERS** on!

This book makes an attempt to address some new questions that have rarely been asked but should be. In 2004, a new women's health medical textbook called ***The Medical & Surgical Practice of* NaPro-TECHNOLOGY**® was published. This book evaluated the medical questions regarding the healthcare of women that are largely left for oral contraceptives, abortion and *in vitro* fertilization to solve. And yet, in spite of their widespread use, these latter approaches have not solved these medical issues and one could argue that they have actually gotten worse over this period of time (Figure Intro-1).

2004

Disturbing Trends in the Health Care of Women, Children and Families

Thomas W. Hilgers, MD

It is truly an honor to be an obstetrician-gynecologist and to work in the field of reproductive medicine. Physicians in this specialty attend to the unique health-care needs of women. They deliver babies in a way which is safe for both the mother and the child. They perform surgical procedures and correct underlying abnormalities and difficulties, and they provide medications that can also cure certain problems or diseases. This is an exceptional privilege. In fact, being a physician, no matter what the specialty might be, is itself a remarkable opportunity.

In reproductive medicine, over the last several centuries,

While there continues to be some progress made in all of these areas, some *truly disturbing trends* observed in the health care of women, children and families have developed, over the last 40+ years. It is vital that these trends be examined and reflected upon so that actions can be taken to reverse them.

The Divorce Rate

In the United States, beginning in the early 1960s, a significant increase in the divorce rate and in the number of children who have been involved in divorce

Figure Intro-1: Opening chapter heading from: Hilgers, TW: The Medical and Surgical Practice of NaProTechnology, Pope Paul VI Institute Press, Omaha, Nebraska, 2004.

This book takes an objective look at data that has been produced by mostly government-based statistical gathering systems, some published in peer-reviewed medical journals and even some in news reports. Because of that, it may be a difficult book to read for some because it is largely a group of statistical tables and graphs, and many people are somewhat afraid to get into this type of data. But if we are going to ask certain types of questions, then we need to look for the answers. Commentary is provided on the statistics and this should help the reader in their understanding.

So the data that is presented in this book comes largely from the following sources: The National Survey for Family Growth, various medical journals, Planned Parenthood's annual reports, the U.S. Census Bureau, Statistical Abstracts of the United States, the Center for Disease Control (CDC) — Assisted Reproductive Technology national reports, various internet sites, the Pregnancy Mortality Surveillance Data collected by the CDC along with the Abortion Surveillance Data, National Vital Statistics Reports, data from the March of Dimes, the United States Agency for International Development, the National Cancer Institute, the National Health Interview Survey and even some data from the Poland Central Statistics Office and the de Veber Institute for Bioethics and Social Research along with various news reports from the Washington Post, USA Today and others. This data is objective and while it has been published, it has rarely been looked at from a collective perspective as a group of data that may have a linkage one to the other.

The reader might ask why would somebody conduct a search and evaluation such as this? The answer lies in the very nature of research. In order to conduct research one has to have a question that needs to be asked. The analysis of the answer to that question, put together from the assessment of the collected data, can provide a scientific assessment which can give new direction to what had been seemingly age-old problems. But the questions that we ask are the result of the values we hold. The medical profession as a general rule, especially those involved in obstetrics, gynecology, reproductive medicine and surgery, have not been interested in the questions addressed in this book. Their ethics and values have become utilitarian and based in relativism. The questions asked are related to the values that many people hold, including many women, but they are no longer held by the overwhelming majority of physicians who take care of women's healthcare needs. These are questions that I ask because I have been dedicated throughout my medical and research life to looking for new solutions, getting to the root cause of the problem and eventually uncovering approaches that have not been thought of, been ignored or purposely left behind (**neglected**).

So in many ways this book is easy to read because it presents data from objective sources which actually can be looked at even if you're not a scientist and it can be evaluated. Most importantly, it is a group of data that needs to be seen in its collective sense although many times an individual set of data has itself its own very serious message. This book eventually comes to the conclusion that we are dealing with one of the biggest public health crises in our nation's history and the history of the Western World. In order to resolve the crisis, new questions must be asked and new answers must be found. It's not just about "poverty and hopelessness" but so many other things. Ultimately, I believe, it comes down to our very sense of freedom and the role that responsibility and irresponsibility play in developing truly legitimate and authentic applications of freedom.

Thomas W. Hilgers, MD

Thomas W. Hilgers, MD
Senior Medical Consultant
Obstetrics, Gynecology, Reproductive
    Medicine and Surgery
Clinical Professor
Department of Obstetrics and
    Gynecology
Creighton University School of
    Medicine
Director
Pope Paul VI Institute for the Study of
    Human Reproduction
Omaha, Nebraska
U.S.A.

CHAPTER 1:

Contraception, Abortion, and IVF: The Medical and Legal Roadmap

In the mid-1950s, following World War II and the Korean War, a magazine was published that sparked a hedonistic (a behavior based on the belief that pleasure is the most important thing in life) "revolution." It took a slightly different approach than what had previously been done in this area by containing written articles and interviews that were thought to be "intellectually stimulating." For those who aspire to intellectualism, it may have made an impact of sorts, but its success wasn't much related to its intellectualism. Women were posed nude and in provocative positions. But Hugh Hefner promised that this was just the beginning of "a sexual revolution" where there would be "no victims" and only pleasure and successful relationships. When he died in 2017, newspapers wrote that he had proclaimed that he had sexual relations with more than 1,000 women. The "Sex without

Love" era had begun! But few of these women are remembered for his exploitations. This was followed by the "sex without kids" dogma of Cosmopolitan's founder, Helen Gurley Brown. Love and life had been separated and the "revolution" produced a large number of victims in its path.

In 1960, the first oral contraceptive was approved by the Food & Drug Administration and instantaneously the birth control pill was prescribed to literally millions of women by their physicians. Along the way, and without direct medical evidence, the birth control pill was promoted to also be helpful in the treatment of a variety of different women's health conditions the cause of which were unknown. So if you had severe menstrual cramps, irregular cycles, abnormal bleeding, recurrent ovarian cysts, endometriosis, pelvic pain of other causes, etc, etc, the first thing the gynecologist (or family doctor) did was put you on birth control pills. This became so prominent that it influenced, even people of faith, that the oral contraceptive was a good thing because it had so many "health benefits." Today, it's actually promoted more on its "health benefits" than it is as a contraceptive, but the direct, well-designed medical evidence is still lacking. Ultimately it is a symptomatic approach to "treatment" that does not get to the root causes.

Table 1-1: The Medical and Legal Roadmap

Item	Year Introduced
Sexually Explicit Material	1955
Oral Contraceptive	1960
Griswold v. Connecticut	1967
Roe v. Wade	1973
First IVF Baby	1978

In 1967, a case involving contraception went to the United States Supreme Court in *Griswold v. Connecticut*. In this decision, the court discovered a new "privacy" right which didn't actually exist in the Constitution. Justice Harry Blackmun, who later wrote one of the most intellectually dishonest opinions in the history of the Supreme Court in *Roe v. Wade* (more on this at a later time), said that the privacy right was found in the "penumbra of the Constitution." But there is techni-cally no penumbra in the Constitution. That belongs with the moon, but the "discovery" of "privacy" was one of the main legal arguments that the U.S. Supreme Court used to validate abortion on demand through virtually the entire course of pregnancy and it became a way of life in the United States of America.

Shortly on its heels, the first *in vitro* fertilization (IVF) baby was born (1978) and all of a sudden the problem of infertility seemed to have been "solved." Of course, it wasn't solved! This was an approach that skipped over the causes of infertility and left women with the diseases that caused the infertility to begin with. In today's world, over 60% of women age 15 to 44 years are using contraception and the use of "the pill" was followed by sterilization, intrauterine devices, con-doms and other contraceptive methods (Figure 1-1).

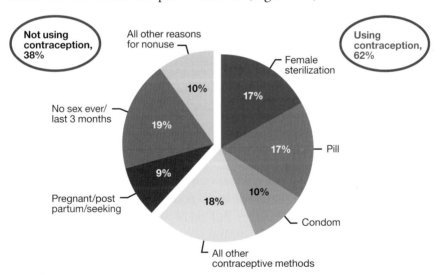

SOURCES: CDC/NCHS, National Survey of Family Growth, 2006-2010.

Figure 1-1: Percent distribution of women aged 15-44 years, by whether they are using contraception and by reasons for nonuse and methods used: United States, 2006–2010.

One manufacturer of the birth control pill eventually decided that they would do a study comparing the effectiveness of oral contracep-tives (their oral contraceptive) to a placebo for teenage acne (Figure 1-2). It had actually been known for a long time that one's skin com-plexion can improve during the time that a young woman takes birth control pills; but it had never been studied with a proper study design.

So this study, which was basically a simple study convinced the

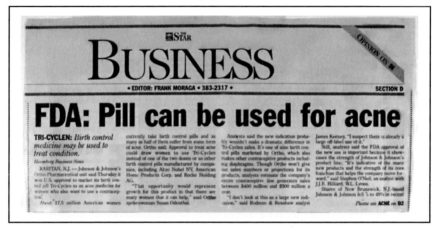

Figure 1-2: FDA Announcement of birth control pill that can be used to treat teenage acne.

Food & Drug Administration that this one birth control pill could label itself as a pill that could be used for acne. Literally, overnight, this pill became the number one selling birth control pill in the world and it maintains that status to a great extent today. This is in spite of the fact that the oral contraceptive, while working in a number of different ways, also works on the lining of the uterus creating an endometrial dysfunction, the dysfunction of various endometrial vessels and other changes (Table 1-2). These effects were ones that would interfere with implantation and could label the birth control pill as, at the very minimum, potentially abortifacient. But there was no going back and the pill became established with almost no self-reflection. **In fact, it was historically the first medical intervention that was used in otherwise healthy women by creating its own physiologically abnormal condition.**

Table 1-2: Mechanism of Action

Endometrial atrophy, change in function of endometrial vessels and other changes in the endometrium (effects that interfere with implantation; abortifacient).

- Combined oral contraceptive
- Progestin only BCP
- Implant devices
- Vaginal ring
- Contraceptive patch
- Progestin Injectables
- IUDs
- Emergency "contraceptives"

As the birth control pill evolved and blood clots were associated with its use and women died, the manufacturers lowered the dose of the estrogen component and sometimes the progestational component. But deep vein thrombosis and venous thromboembolism both — even in low-dose oral contraceptives — were still significantly increased in its users. Whenever you hear of a young woman who was otherwise in good health dies for apparently no reason, you need to always think immediately of the birth control pill and its effect. In fact, more often than not, that woman was taking "the pill" and had a venous thromboembolic event that, for her, was fatal.

The medical profession was left with still uncertain and really important questions. For example, how do we get teenagers to actually take this pill on a regular basis since being noncompliant was a major problem? So one of the journals published a randomized controlled trial in which daily text-message reminders were sent to improve adherence with the use of the oral contraceptive. However, daily text-message reminders, (which one would think would be perfect for this millennial generation), did not improve oral contraceptive pill adherence (Figure 1-3).

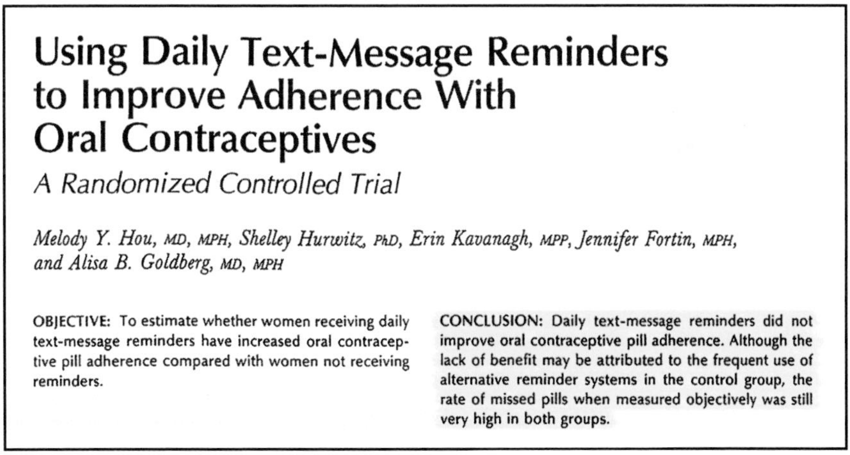

Using Daily Text-Message Reminders to Improve Adherence With Oral Contraceptives

A Randomized Controlled Trial

Melody Y. Hou, MD, MPH, Shelley Hurwitz, PhD, Erin Kavanagh, MPP, Jennifer Fortin, MPH, and Alisa B. Goldberg, MD, MPH

OBJECTIVE: To estimate whether women receiving daily text-message reminders have increased oral contraceptive pill adherence compared with women not receiving reminders.

CONCLUSION: Daily text-message reminders did not improve oral contraceptive pill adherence. Although the lack of benefit may be attributed to the frequent use of alternative reminder systems in the control group, the rate of missed pills when measured objectively was still very high in both groups.

Figure 1-3: Daily text message reminders did not improve oral contraceptive adherence. (Obstet Gynecol 2010; 116:633–640).

There has been a lot of discussion given lately to the topic of the taxpayer funding for Planned Parenthood (Figure 1-4). There has been over a 500% increase in the funding of Planned Parenthood between 1987 and 2015. In the Clinton administration in the early 1990s and overwhelmingly so with the Obama administration, the funding was increased significantly. The reader should be reminded that the ultimate goal of Margaret Sanger was the targeting of low-income groups and especially black Americans. But with Obama, a black president, it wasn't questioned.

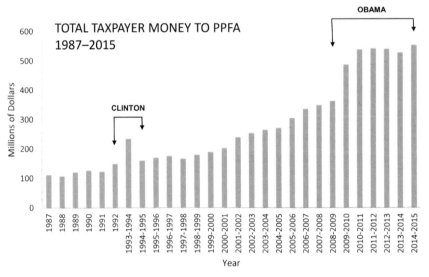

Figure 1-4: The federal funding of Planned Parenthood from 1987 through 2014–2015
Citation: Gigant K: Your Tax Dollars at Work for Planned Parenthood. Celebrate Life. 25:42–45
PPFA Annual Report 2002, 2003, 2004, 2005, 2006, 2007, 2008, 2009, 2010, 2012, 2013, 2014

As you read this book, you're going to come across a number of graphs that look generically like the one in Figure 1-5. This graph shows the occurrence of some factor that moves from a relatively low incidence to a relatively high incidence over a relatively short period of time. This is called "the shift" and it has a Point A which is basically the beginning of that shift upwards and a Point B where it begins to stabilize at the higher rate. Many of the things in this book will refer to that shift — it is a shift in the frequency of occurrence to a higher rate or more frequent occurrence of the cited issues.

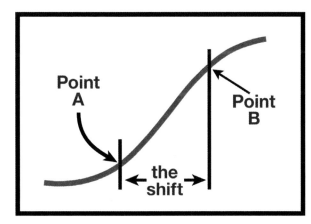

Figure 1-5: The shift in many of the events cited is exponential with a Point A and a Point B.

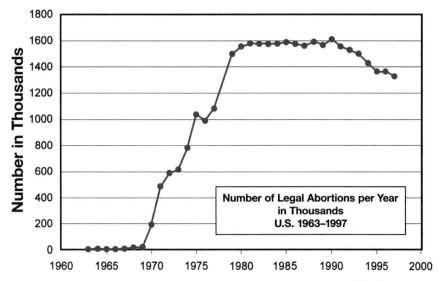

Figure 1-6: The number of legal abortions per year in the thousands, United States, 1963–1997. Updated Source: U.S. Census Bureau, Statistical Abstract of the United States: 2012

So, in Figure 1-6, we have the number of legal abortions in the United States from 1963-1997. Before the late 1960s, abortion was largely illegal in the United States and there were very few performed. While arguing that 5,000 to 10,000 women died each year in the United States by illegal abortion and that there were a million illegal abortions every year in the United States, these statistics were made up by an organization called the National Association for the Repeal of Abortion Laws (NARAL) and was revealed by one of its co-founders,

Dr. Bernard Nathanson. There actually is extremely good national data on the number of women who died from abortion-related causes (all causes) providing support to the premise that these numbers were greatly exaggerated!

In today's world, it's a little bit more complicated because the number of abortions being recorded has decreased since the mid-1990s and many different groups including different groups that speak in defense of life accept the notion that the number of abortions is decreasing. However, they often don't take into account the fact that many abortions are performed with medications such as the use of the French abortion pill RU-486. In some news accounts, this represents about 25% of all abortions in the United States and seriously questions whether or not the number of abortions is decreasing. Furthermore, abortions which were associated with *in vitro* fertilization and/or the use of various contraceptives such as the oral contraceptive and intra-uterine device are not taken into account at all (Figure 1-7).

Incidence of Medical Abortion

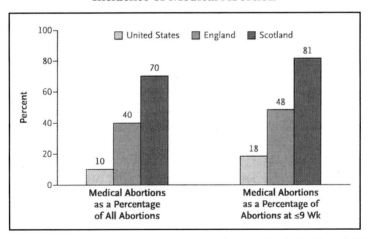

Figure 1-7. Medical Abortion in the United States, England, and Scotland, New England Journal of Medicine.

We see another graph in Figure 1-8 and this shows the implementation of technological forms of contraception, especially the oral contraceptive, and how that increased rapidly after its introduction in 1960 and preceded the exponential rise in the number of abortions by about 8 years. This strongly suggests that there is a connection between the increased use of contraceptive agents which also triggered a change in the moral compass of people who bought into the idea that there were "no victims" — only pleasure. This is actually a convenient argument which on very superficial reflection would seem to suggest that that is what would happen. And yet, truly the opposite has happened. The so-called "sexual revolution" has built a road that is littered with victims. Instead of preventing abortion, the widespread use of contraceptive agents led to an increase in the number of abortions. The argument that we need contraception to reduce the number of abortions (a common political argument) is virtually without foundation.

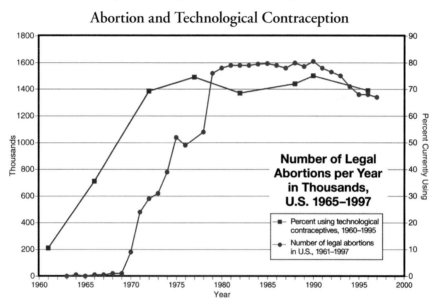

Figure 1-8: The number of legal abortions per year in the United States and the percentage of women age 15-44 using technological contraceptives.

Couples who have infertility problems yearn deeply for a child. So with the advent of abortion with one of the calling cards, "every child a wanted child," the introduction of the artificial reproductive technologies, most especially various forms of *in vitro* fertilization (IVF) produced a whole new class of victims. I know this because the great part of my own medical practice is devoted to the evaluation and treatment of the root medical causes of infertility.

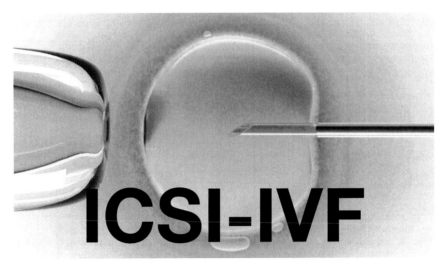

Figure 1-9: Intracytoplasmic sperm injection (ICSI) IVF. From: OB-GYN News, May 2017

Many of the women that I see are struck by the fertility abuse that occurs in our culture with contraception, abortion, sterilization and IVF. They're also struck by the young teenager, not married, who seems to have no difficulty getting pregnant in what otherwise is a fatherless relationship. And then they are told by the IVF doctor that "the only way you will get pregnant is with IVF." In their hands that's likely a true statement, but it is not true when other specialists become involved with their care. We've had patients following failures of *in vitro* fertilization who become pregnant simply with the use of the days in the cycle that are most fertile. Not a complicated treatment and certainly not one that is difficult to implement.

Table 1-3: Embryo Loss Ratio (ELR): IVF[1] in the United States 2000 – 2011

	Numbers	%
Total Embryos Established	3,296,370	100.0
Total Live Births	471,087	14.3
Total Infants	628,733	19.1
Embryo Loss	2,667,637	80.9
Embryo Loss Ratio (ELR): IVF	4.2:1.0[2]	

1. Calculated from: Assisted Reproductive Technology National Summary Reports for 2000 – 2011, Atlanta (GA): U.S. Dept. of Health and Human Services, 2013.
2. 4.2 embryos lost for every one live birth.

And then it is becoming more and more well known that there are a large number of early embryos that are lost through the IVF process. Our own calculations from the National Data Summaries of the Center for Disease Control in cooperation with the Society of Assisted Reproductive Technology indicates that the ratio of embryo loss to one IVF baby born is 4.2:1.0 or 2,667,637 embryos lost from 2000 to 2011 alone (Table 1-3). This is 80.9% of all embryos generated. It is because of this that many people do not want to even take a look at IVF. They do not want to be a part of such a cold, calculating and insensitive process. And in reality, the total number of cycles of IVF that were performed in the United States in 2013 was about 160,000. But there are 9.5 million women every year who have reproductive issues that need some treatment. And yet, the IVF approach helps less than 0.5% of those women; and of course it doesn't do anything related to the underlying causes (Figure 1-10).

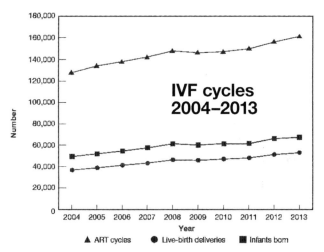

Figure 1-10: Numbers of Performed, Live-Birth Deliveries, and Infants Born Using IVF, 2004–2013.

The cost of these procedures is also very expensive. The multi-center median for a couple's expense with IVF over only one cycle of treatment is $19,000 (out of pocket) and if the woman needs "donor eggs," it doubles to over $39,000 per cycle (Table 1-4). If a couple utilizes artificial insemination (which has a notoriously poor success rate), while also being divisive to the marriage relationship, has a per-cycle cost in the $600-$900 range (Table 1-5).

Table 1-4: Out of pocket expense for In-Vitro Fertilization (IVF)[1] 2015

Reproductive Associates of Colorado	Cost per cycle
Total fresh cycle	$16,851 – $19,351
Total frozen cycle	$14,851 – $15,851
Advanced Fertility Center, Chicago	
One IVF cycle with monitoring	$12,000 – $13,500
Multicenter Median	
Overall Couple Expense — IVF	$19,234
Overall IVF with donor eggs	$39,197

1. From major provider internet sites, 2015.

Table 1-5: Out of Pocket Expense for Artificial Insemination[1] 2015

Resolve.org	Cost
IUI[2] single cycle	$865
California Cryobank	
Intracervical cycle	$595 – $695
Intrauterine cycle	$695 – $795

1. From major provider internet sites, 2015.
2. IUI = Intrauterine Sperm Insemination.

There are some additional really outlandish parts of this industry. In Figure 1-11 and 1-12 are two advertisements on embryo storage programs. The first reads, "Embryonic Storage Headaches? Choose one of these and call us in the morning." The other one reads, "Who's Watching the Kids?" This is a profession which continues to deny that they are working with living human beings, except when they are selling something they consider to be important, valuable, and lucrative.

Figure 1-11: IVF related Advertisement

Figure 1-11: IVF related Advertisement

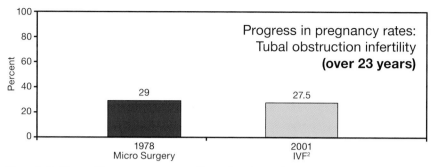

Figure 1-12: "Progress" in pregnancy rates over 23 years in patients with tubal factor infertility. In 1978, micro-surgical correction of tubal adhesions resulted in a 29 percent "per woman" pregnancy rate. Later, the live birth per cycle started with IVF was 27.5.

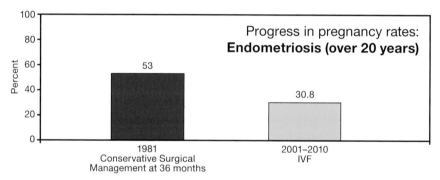

Figure 1-13: "Progress" in the development of pregnancies over 20 years in patients with endometriosis. In 1981, 53.9 percent of patients achieved pregnancy over 36 months ("per woman") with conservative surgical management. Later, the pregnancy rate per cycle started with IVF was 30.8.

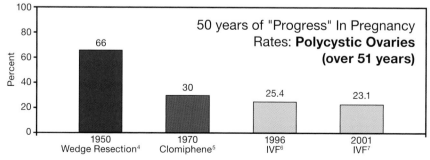

Figure 1-14: Fifty years of "progress" in pregnancy rates in patients with polycystic ovarian disease. In 1950, the pregnancy rate from wedge resection was 66 percent. In 2001, the pregnancy rate per cycle started with IVF was 23.1, in 2017 wedge resection was up to 75–80 percent.

There are a couple of other questions that are important to be asked in all of this. While *in vitro* fertilization would appear to be — from news reports — the only successful treatment for infertility, a look at the success of other approaches — aimed at trying to correct the underlying diseases is very revealing. In Figures 1-12, 1-13 and 1-14 the question is asked whether any progress has been made over the last 40-60 years with regard to pregnancy rates in women who have different organic or hormonal causes for their infertility. For example, the microsurgical treatment of tubal obstruction in 1978 carried with it a 29% success rate. When IVF was measured against it 20 years later, the pregnancy rate was 27.5%. Both of these may have increased over the last 16 years, however, surgical correction of the obstruction continues to be more effective as well.

What about endometriosis? With surgical correction of endometriosis, the pregnancy rate was 53% in 1981. In 2001, it was 29 percent and with more recent data, it's up to 30% with IVF. And with polycystic ovarian disease, in 1950, with surgical correction, the pregnancy rate was 66%. There is not a study that has been done with *in vitro* fertilization that exceeds 30%. The important point here is that probably **for the first time in medical history, the medical profession substituted a less effective treatment for what was previously a more effective treatment.** There's a gross injustice here. I tell my patients that "If this were AIDS and this approach to treatment was undertaken … all hell would break loose!" And yet, with women who have infertility, who only want to improve their chances of finding the cause and achieving a pregnancy, the medical profession not only looks away from them, but looks to treatment approaches that are not only expensive, but they don't treat the underlying diseases and are markedly less effective. Infertility patients need their own lobby so they can lobby for better approaches that are aimed at treating the underlying causes.

There are other significant drawbacks to the *in vitro* fertilization approach. For example, children conceived by IVF procedures are at significantly increased risk for birth defects (Figure 1-15). Admissions for early parenting difficulties among women who conceived with IVF are also increased compared to spontaneous conception (Figure 1-16).

Birth defects in children conceived by in vitro fertilization and intracytoplasmic sperm injection: a meta-analysis

Juan Wen, B.S.,[a,b] Jie Jiang, B.S.,[a,b] Chenyue Ding, B.S.,[a,b] Junchang Dai, M.D.,[b] Yao Liu, B.S.,[b] Yankai Xia, M.D., Ph.D.,[a,c] Jiayin Liu, M.D., Ph.D.,[a,d] and Zhibin Hu, M.D., Ph.D.[a,b]

[a] State Key Laboratory of Reproductive Medicine, [b] Department of Epidemiology and Biostatistics, [c] Department of Toxicology, Key Laboratory of Modern Toxicology of Ministry of Education, School of Public Health, and [d] Center of Clinical Reproductive Medicine, the First Affiliated Hospital, Nanjing Medical University, Nanjing, People's Republic of China

Objective: To conduct a meta-analysis of studies assessing the effect of IVF and intracytoplasmic sperm injection (ICSI) on birth defects.
Design: Meta-analysis.
Setting: Centers for reproductive care.
Patient(s): Patients treated by IVF and/or ICSI.
Intervention(s): We identified all studies published by September 2011 with data related to birth defects in children conceived by IVF and/or ICSI compared with spontaneously conceived children, or birth defects in the children conceived by IVF compared with those by ICSI. Risk ratios from individual studies were pooled with the fixed and random effect models.
Main Outcome Measure(s): Risk of birth defects in children conceived by IVF and/or ICSI.
Result(s): Of 925 studies reviewed for eligibility, 802 were excluded after screening titles and abstracts, 67 were excluded for duplicated data, data unavailable, or inappropriate control group, 56 were included in the final analysis. Among the 56 studies, 46 studies had data on birth defects in children conceived by IVF and/or ICSI (134,468) compared with spontaneously conceived children. These studies provided a pooled risk estimation of 1.37 (95% confidence interval [CI]: 1.26–1.48), which is also evident in subgroup analysis. In addition, 24 studies had data on birth defects in children conceived by IVF (46,890) compared with those by ICSI (27,754), which provided an overall no risk difference.
Conclusion(s): Children conceived by IVF and/or ICSI are at significantly increased risk for birth defects, and there is no risk difference between children conceived by IVF and/or ICSI. (Fertil Steril® 2012;97:1331–7. ©2012 by American Society for Reproductive Medicine.)
Key Words: Birth defects, IVF, ICSI, meta-analysis

Children conceived by IVF and/or ICSI are at significantly increased risk for birth defects, and there is no risk difference between children conceived by IVF and/or ICSI. (Fertil Steril® 2012; 97: 1331-7).

Figure 1-15

ORIGINAL ARTICLE: MENTAL HEALTH, SEXUALITY, AND ETHICS

Admissions for early parenting difficulties among women with infants conceived by assisted reproductive technologies: a prospective cohort study

Jane R. W. Fisher, Ph.D.,[a,b] Heather Rowe, Ph.D.,[a,b] and Karin Hammarberg, Ph.D.[a,b]

[a] Jean Hailes Research Unit, School of Public Health and Preventive Medicine, Monash University, Clayton; and [b] Centre for Women's Health Gender and Society, Melbourne School of Population Health, University of Melbourne, Melbourne, Victoria, Australia

Objective: To describe rate of and risks for residential early parenting service (REPS) admissions in women with infants conceived with assisted reproductive technology (ART).
Design: A prospective study of women who conceived with ART. Self-report telephone interview and questionnaire data were collected in two pregnancy and three postpartum waves.
Setting: Melbourne IVF and Royal Women's Hospital Reproductive Services, Victoria, Australia.
Patient(s): A consecutive cohort of women with ART pregnancies.
Intervention(s): None.
Main Outcome Measure(s): REPS admission up to 18 months postpartum.
Result(s): Of 239 eligible women, 185 (77%) were recruited, six experienced pregnancy loss, and 153 (77%) (86%) were retained. In total, 17% (24/153) of participants were admitted to a REPS. 3.3V times more than the population admission rate of 5.05%. Admission risk was increased by primiparity, inadequate breastfeeding advice, low caregiving confidence when discharged from maternity hospital, lower early postpartum mood, unsettled infant behavior, and insufficient help from others.
Conclusion(s): Compared with spontaneous conception, women who conceived with ART are at elevated risk of early parenting difficulties. Early interventions to address breastfeeding difficulties, management of unsettled infant behavior, social isolation, and postpartum anxiety are indicated. (Fertil Steril® 2012;97:1410–6. ©2012 by American Society for Reproductive Medicine.)
Key Words: Assisted reproductive technology, women, postpartum admission, parenting services, unsettled infant behavior

Compared with spontaneous conception, women who conceived with ART are at elevated risk of early parenting difficulties. (Fertil Steril® 2012; 97: 1410-6).

Figure 1-16

So the highway that is littered with victims of the medical profession continues to grow. I haven't even mentioned the euphemistic expression "selective reduction" which takes a baby that is desperately wanted by a woman with an infertility problem and aborts it by injecting its heart with poison (potassium chloride) when there are multiple babies in utero.

CHAPTER 2:

Maternal Mortality
1775 – 2013

It has always been a great joy for me to take care of women who are pregnant and to deliver their babies. I've always felt that I was a member of a profession that was especially graced by the opportunity to provide safe healthcare for women who are pregnant. I had a cousin's mother who died in childbirth and that really wasn't all that long ago. I have told a number of people over the years that things can happen more quickly in the delivery room than perhaps any place in medicine (and that would include the emergency room and the operating room). In Figure 2-1, you can see the reduction in the incidence of women who have died in childbirth from the year 1775 all the way up through 2013. A great deal of progress has been made in this field over these last 200+ years with rapid improvement in the last century. I have personally been blessed by not ever having a woman die as a result of her pregnancy. But there have been, indeed, very complex situations. Having said that, while the profession has made great strides in this particular area, the very concept of maternal death has now been used against them.

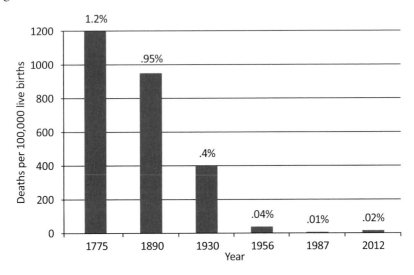

Figure 2-1: Maternal Mortality in Deaths per 100,000 live Births. Data from the US only. Previous data may or may not be from the United States only (see below).

For data from 1987 to 2012: Center for Disease Control and Prevention. Pregnancy Mortality Surveillance System. U.S Department of Health and Human Services. January 21, 2016. http://www.cdc.gov/reproductivehealth/maternalinfanthealth/pmss.html

For data from 1775–1956: Gibbs RS: Impact of Infectious Diseases on Women's Health: 1776-2026, Obstet Gynecol 97:1019-1023, 2001. Gibbs RS does not specify whether data is from the US only. Their sources for this data are: Shorter E. A History of Women's Bodies. New York: Basic Books, 1982.

Bureau of the Census with the Cooperation of the Social Service Research Council. Historical statistics of the United States, colonial times to 1957. Washington DC: United States Government Printing Office, 1960.

Leavitt JW. Brought to bed. Childbearing in America, 1750-1950. New York: Oxford University Press, 1986.

In the lead up to *Roe v. Wade* it was argued that, as I had indicated earlier, there were 5,000 to 10,000 maternal deaths per year due to illegal abortion, and yet as one goes through the data on these years, there is **absolutely no evidence** of that, only the admission that it was fabricated. In Figure 2-2, the maternal mortality rates from 1960 through 1978 in the United States are shown. The beginning of legalized abortion (1968), the first marked increase in abortion in the United States (1970) and the impact of *Roe v. Wade* (1973) are all noted and yet there's been no dramatic decline in maternal mortality because of the implementation of legal abortion. If there were, in fact, thousands upon thousands of women who died from illegal abortion, an abrupt decrease would show up in this data after legalization.

Instead, the decrease continued at the well-established rate that existed before abortion was legalized. Legalization had no impact.

One of the foundational medical assumptions in *Roe v. Wade* which was promoted to the Court by the American College of Obstetricians & Gynecologists was that childbirth was 23.3 times more dangerous than that of first trimester abortion. They arrived at these numbers by taking the maternal mortality rate in the United States, which a few years prior to *Roe v. Wade* was 28.0 per 100,000 and comparing it to the maternal mortality rate in Hungary for first trimester abortion which was listed at 1.2 per 100,000. If you divide those two numbers, the 23.3 times number is reached.

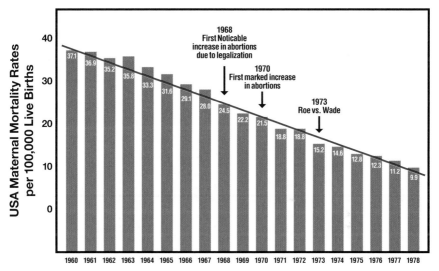

Figure 2-2: Maternal Mortality Rates — USA 1960–1978 (From: Maternal Mortality Statistics, National Center for Health Statistics, 1960–1978)

Roe v. Wade indicated that "maternal mortality" from "**ordinary**" or "**normal**" childbirth is 23.3 times more dangerous than that of first trimester abortion. I have spent a lifetime trying to address these statistics and I must admit and even apologize for the fact that I have never been very successful at doing this. Having said that, however, I now know the mistake that I made. The United States Supreme Court accepted the notion that "**maternal mortality**" from "**ordinary**" or "**normal**" childbirth was extremely high compared to abortion and yet the maternal mortality rate from "**ordinary**" or "**normal**" childbirth is **actually zero!** If there is a maternal death in childbirth or from pregnancy it is due to a catastrophic medical occurrence of some sort. It was far from "normal" or "ordinary."

Shortly after *Roe v. Wade* when I spent a lot of time with this data, I didn't see the terms "ordinary" or "normal" — even though it was there — I missed the point completely. The reason I did, however, was because I had in my mind a certain sense that the United States Supreme Court and the American College were trying to be honest with the American people and I just did not suspect deceit or "fake" science like this. Now, I know differently. I know from the political struggles that are currently ongoing in the United States that lying, deceit, and falsification of data has almost become a way of life. While many at the time of *Roe v. Wade* were up in arms because of this high rate of maternal mortality associated with "ordinary" or "normal" childbirth, there hasn't been much said since that time.

Maternal deaths

Women are dying from childbirth at the highest rate in decades, according to recent government figures.

Maternal mortality,
per 100,000 live births

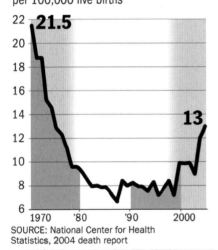

SOURCE: National Center for Health Statistics, 2004 death report

THE ASSOCIATED PRESS

Figure 2-3: Increasing rate of maternal mortality in the U.S.

In the early part of the 21st century, reports were beginning to be published that the maternal mortality rate was starting to increase again after it had dropped to an all-time low in the 1990s (Figure 2-3). In 2017, data for the maternal mortality in the United States from 1999 until 2013 was published in *OB-GYN News* citing data from the Center for Disease Control & Prevention. In this case, the maternal mortality rate in the United States had reached 22 per 100,000. So, if you were to take the maternal mortality rate *without* nationalized abortion in 1972 (the figure that was known and available for 1972 18.8 per 100,000) and compare it to the data in 2013, *with* a nationalized abortion program in the United States, this rate had increased to 22.0 per 100,000. In other words, the maternal mortality rate *with* legalized abortion had **increased** and now was **1.17 times greater**. And yet, there is no outcry from those people who promote abortion as there was in the early 1970s. There is no outcry from the American College of Obstetricians and Gynecologists as there was with their *amicus* brief to the United States Supreme Court. In addition, there's no outcry from anybody who listed their name on that *amicus* brief.

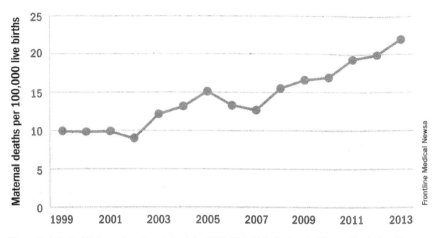

Figure 2-4: United States maternal mortality data, 1999–2013, U.S. Centers for Disease Control and Prevention as cited in Ob. Gyn. News, January, 2017.

This raises a significant question; and that question is "Do these people really care?" More and more, it begins to appear that they do not.

In vitro fertilization also carries with it a mortality rate. Conditions like ovarian hyperstimulation syndrome (OHSS) can be a fatal complication of IVF programs. In addition, venous thromboembolism also

Table 2-3: Death with IVF

- Women have also died from IVF: OHSS and venous thromboembolism.
- The exact ratios are not known.

OHSS = Ovarian Hyperstimulation Syndrome

occurs with IVF, but the exact ratios of both of these are not known at this time. It should be noted that nobody to our knowledge has died from any of the services that we have provided (Table 2-3).

CHAPTER 3 :

Infant and Embryonic/ Fetal Mortality

It is well known that the infant mortality rate in the United States is significantly higher than in a number of developed nations from around the world (Figure 3-1). The infant mortality rate in the United States was 6.1 per 1,000 live births and in Japan, for example, it was 2.3; in Germany, it was 3.4; Italy 3.4; France 3.6; Ireland 3.8; Australia 4.1; the UK 4.2; and in Poland 5.0 (2010).

The main cause of these infant deaths is due to prematurity as shown in Figure 3-2. The infant deaths are to a great extent related to low birth weight and congenital malformations. Prematurity is often related to multiple births. With the increasing rate of *in vitro* fertilization, the number of multiple births has increased (Figure 3-3). And it has climbed every year since 1980.

There are also increased infant deaths depending upon the type of multiple birth. Twins, triplets and quadruplets actually increase significantly the infant mortality for those babies (and in that order)

(Figure 3-4). The national multiple pregnancy rate in the IVF programs is about 32%, while with the approach that we have taken in the treatment of infertility, it is 3.2% or 10 times lower.

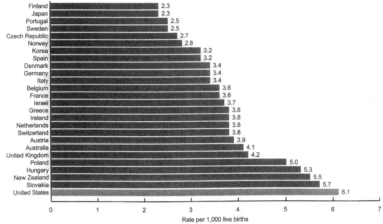

Figure 3-1: Infant mortality rates: Selected for Economic Co-operation and Development countries, 2010* *From: National Vital Statistics Reports, September 24, 2014

In Figure 3-5, we have a number of different mortality rates that are identified. Both the infant mortality and fetal mortality are in the lower portion of the graph. While it indicates that both are decreasing, there's **a major flaw in the data.** It's like they're trying to hide something. In actual fact, the number in these rates **specifically exclude deaths due to induced abortion or in vitro fertilization embryo deaths.** So the actual fetal mortality rate is significantly higher than this.

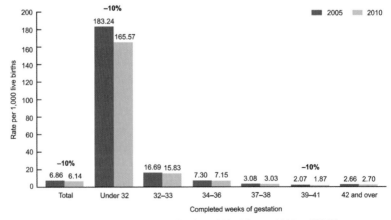

Figure 3-2: Infant mortality rates, by gestational age: United States, 2005 and 2010*
*From: National Vital Statistics Reports, December 18, 2013

That would also include the perinatal mortality rate if you calculated it separately with the addition of abortions that are late-term events.

In Figure 3-5, a graph which shows the IVF embryo mortality rates per 1,000 IVF births. While this has decreased since these numbers were calculated, they are still extremely high and completely unacceptable.

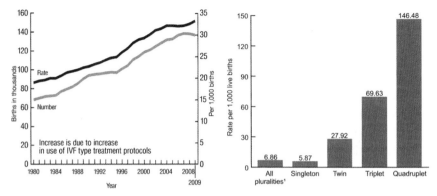

Figure 3-3: Number and rate of twin births: United States, 1980–2009. SOURCE: CDC/NCHS, National Center for Health Statistics, Data Brief, January 2012.

Figure 3-4: Infant mortality rates, by plurality: United States, 2006. From: National Vital Statistics Reports, April 30, 2010.

So we actually have formal data on the infant and fetal mortality rate in which they've left out a significant population of fetal deaths in a move that appears to be purposely deceptive. These non-recorded deaths have been purposely left out of the statistics gathered for what are apparently political motives. The fetal deaths from induced abortion have been excluded by the NCVS.

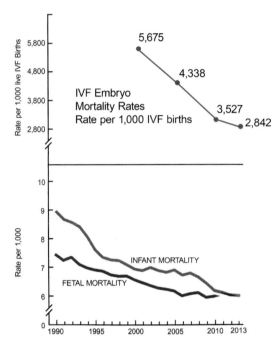

Figure 3-5: Infant mortality rates per 1,000 live births.

Fetal mortality rates are number of fetal deaths at 20 weeks or more per 1,000 live births. These rates specifically exclude deaths due to induced abortion and IVF embryo deaths. IVF embryo mortality rates per 1,000 live IVF births (2000–2013).

National Vital Statistics Reports, Vol. 64, No. 8, July 23, 2015.

Pope Paul VI Institute Research from SART Database.

CHAPTER 4:

Trends in Marriage and Divorce

The number of divorces and the number of children involved in divorce are both shown in Figure 4-1. The ratio of divorce to marriage in any given year is shown in Figure 4-2. There are a couple of important things to note here. First of all, divorce, while being present in the culture during the 1950s and early 1960s started to really increase significantly in the early 1960s and reached its peak in the early 1980s. The number of children being affected by divorce also increases in an exponential way that actually precedes the occurrence of the divorce.

Some have argued that the number of divorces has decreased which, in reality, is true but so have the number of marriages decreased. So the actual ratio of divorce to marriage has remained the same since the early 1970s (Figure 4-2) with an exponential curve beginning in the late 1960s. It has continued to be fairly stable since then, but at the much higher rate.

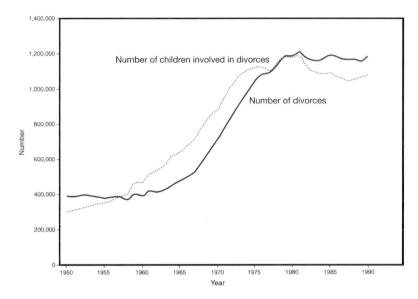

Figure 4-1: The number of divorces and children involved in divorces in the United States; 1950–1990*.

From: Vital and Health Statistics: Supplements to the Monthly Vital statistics Report. Series 24, No. 9, April 2003.

The temporal relationship with the increased use of technological contraception and the increased number of divorces is shown in Figure 4-3 from 1950 through 1990. Again, technological forms of contraception had a huge increase shortly after the birth control pill came out that preceded the increased rate of divorce. There are not many studies that have looked at this relationship, but one such study from the University of Chicago reported a sizeable and robust statistical analysis for the various potential causes of this increase in divorce (Table 4-1).

Table 4-1: Why has the divorce rate increased?

Potential Cause	% Responsible
Changes in divorce laws	NPR
Unemployment	NPR
Military manpower	NPR
Public assistance variables	10
Income Variables	23
Age composition variables	25
Contraception diffusion variable	>50
Unaccounted for	6

NPR = Not Positively Related
Michael RT: Why Did the U.S. Divorce Rate Double Within a Decade?
Research in Population Economics 6:367-399, 1988.

It was found that the standard responses such as change in the divorce laws, unemployment, involvement in the military or public assistance variables were not major forces in this increase. Even such things as income variables or variables in age composition between the spouses contributed only moderately. **The major variable that accounted for the increase in divorce was the introduction, on a widespread scale, of the various contraceptive technologies**, which included mostly the oral contraceptive and intrauterine device and then later female and male sterilization.

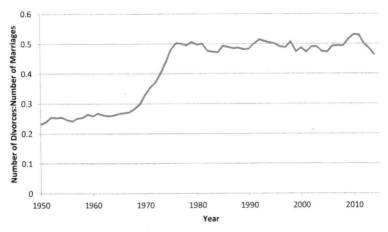

Figure 4-2: Ratio of Divorce to Marriage per Year in the United States from 1950 to 2014*

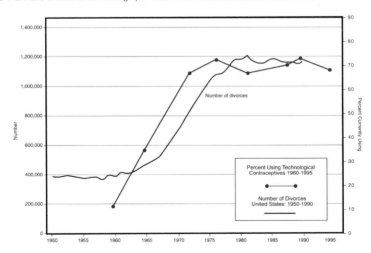

Figure 4-3: The Temporal Relationship with the increase in use of Technological Contraception and the Increase in the Number of Divorces

The percentage of women aged 15 to 45 using technological forms of contraceptives, 1960–1995, and the number of divorces in the United States, 1950–1990.

Over this period of time, the family was hit very hard with the introduction of contraceptive sexual relations. Each of the spouses became the object more of pleasure (Hefner) than of objects of love and unity. Indeed, women became wombs to be deactivated rather than persons with lives to be fulfilled. Men have responded in ways where they are most vulnerable and true sexual meaning appeared to be a mirage!

CHAPTER 5:

Maltreatment of Women and Children

What has happened to the healthcare of women and children during the course of these last 50-60 years? We know that coercion is often involved in induced abortions, sex trafficking has become a major problem, and sex-selection abortions (gendercide) also has become a significant issue (Table 5-1 and 5-2).

Table 5-1: The relationship of abortion and violence against women

- Coerced abortion
- Sex trafficking
- Sex selection abortions ("gendercide")

From: Issues in Law and Medicine, Fall 2015

Table 5-2: In Most Abortions

- Men played a central role in decision to abort.................. 95%
- Inadequate counseling beforehand 84%
- Women wanted to have the baby..83%
- Not counseled about alternatives . 79%
- Involve coercion 64%

1. From: www.afterabortion.org, 2013

Psychiatric admission following abortion is much higher in the times following the abortion compared to women who have delivered a baby and death by suicide after abortion is 6–7 times higher than after childbirth and 3½ times higher than if no pregnancy was involved at all (Figures 5-1 and 5-2). As a followup note to that, the mental health problems of women who had an abortion are also much higher than women who carried to term, women who have not had an abortion and "unintended" pregnancy that was carried to term (Table 5-3). Furthermore, the mental health problems in women who have had an abortion vs. women who have not had an abortion in 22 peer-reviewed studies shows that marijuana use, suicide behaviors, alcohol use and misuse, depression and anxiety are all statistically significantly increased in those women vs. women who had not had an abortion (Table 5-4). The facts about intimate partner violence (IPV) are listed in Table 5-5 and the impact of the father's involvement or non-involvement with their children is detailed in Figure 5-3. If the fathers lived apart from their children, their interaction was truly minimal, but if they lived with their children, the interaction was much greater especially with regard to eating meals and talking about the day.

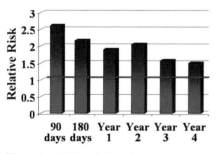
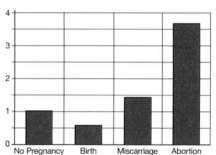

Figure 5-1: Relative Risk of Subsequent Psychiatric Admission for Aborting Women Compared to Delivering Women (RR=1) by Time after Pregnancy Outcome

Figure 5-2: Death by Suicide

Child abuse data is somewhat difficult to find good sources for. This is surprising given the fact that it has been an item of great concern to many people. One can't, however, simply disregard the intrauterine violence that is done to the early embryo and fetus. People have tried to talk about that in our culture, but oftentimes one is not allowed to speak about it. As a gynecologist who is also a surgeon, one realizes how significantly violent the destruction of the embryo is, and for those who have empathy and a sense of connection to the humanity of that child, it truly presents a horrible, violent, and vicious end to their life.

Table 5-3: Mental Health Problems: Women who had an Abortion vs.

	Odds Ratio [1,2]
Women who carried to term	2.38
Women who had not had an abortion	1.59
"Unintended" pregnancy carried to term	1.55

1. In each case, the p-value was <0.0001.
2. From: Coleman PK: Abortion and Mental Health: Quantitative Synthesis and Analysis of Research. Published 1995-2009. Brit J Psych 199:180-186, 2011.

Table 5-4: Mental Health Problems: Women who Had an Abortion vs. Women who Had Not Had an Abortion (22 Peer-reviewed Studies[1])

Symptom	Odds Ratio	p-value
Marijuana use	3.30	0.001
Suicide behaviors	2.55	0.006
Alcohol use/misuse	2.10	<0.0001
Depression	1.37	<0.0001
Anxiety	1.34	<0.0001
Pooled Odds Ratio	**1.81**	**<0.0001**

1. Coleman PK: Abortion and Mental Health: Quantitative Synthesis and Analysis of Research. Published 1995-2009. Brit J Psych 199:180-186, 2011.

Table 5-5: Intimate Partner Violence (IPV): Facts

- Every 9 seconds in the U.S. a woman is assaulted or beaten
- 20 people per minute
- 10 million abuse victims annually
- 1 in 3 women and 1 in 4 men has been physically abused through IPV.
- Domestic violence hotlines receive 20,800 calls daily.
- Domestic violence accounts for 15% of all violent crime.
- IPV increases the rates of depression and suicidal behavior.
- Only 34% of victims receive medical care.
- 8 million days of paid work are lost every year.
- The cost = $83 billion per year.

From NCADV (2015), www.NCADV.org

Figure 5-3: Fathers' Involvement With Their Children

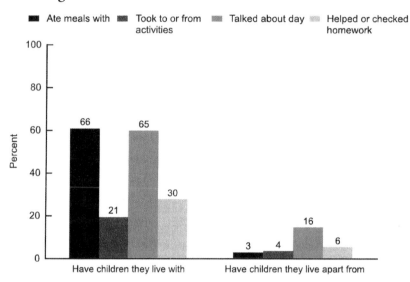

SOURCES: CDC/NCHS, National Survey of Family Growth, 2006-2010.

Percentage of fathers aged 15–44 who have children aged 5–18 years who engaged in the specified activity daily in the last 4 weeks, by whether the children live with or apart from them: United States, 2006-2010

As we look at the violence, which seems to be ever-present in the streets and gathering places of America, one data point is rarely mentioned. There have now been over 60,000,000 abortions performed in the U.S. since it was legalized. The unborn are the most vulnerable and innocent among us and are treated as a non-existing entity, and yet we who are alive currently have *survived our own in utero existence!* This lack of basic respect and protection of the most innocent among us is bound to continue to have a significantly injurious impact.

CHAPTER 6:

Non-Marital Childbearing, Cohabitation, and the "Poverty Gap"

It is common for the people in today's world to look at the number and the rate of children that are born to women who are not married as "declining." In Figure 6-1, the number and rate of non-marital childbearing declined from the 2008 peak and this is noted by the dotted line that runs through the data. And yet, if one goes back further in time to 1940 through 2013, one sees that there is a steep uphill climb in the number of children that were born to unmarried women. In fact, even the birth rate before contraception was extremely low compared to now. Planned Parenthood said that every child should be a wanted child, but if a child is born into a single relationship — a mother only — you can't make a strong argument that that is a wanted child and yet it has increased exponentially during the course of these years. Yes, there has been a slight decrease in the last couple of years, but relative to 1940, 1950, even 1960, it's extremely high. We have a tendency in these statistics not to look back far enough and to believe everything that everybody says, but they're often reflecting only on the last few years. **They are not looking "downstream."** Many people don't know that this data goes back many decades and one can do this type of comparative analysis.

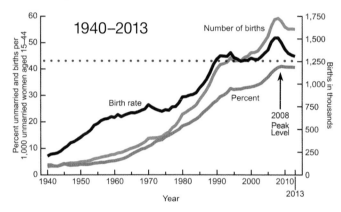

Figure 6-1: "The number and rate of nonmarital childbearing declined from the 2008 peak." NOTE: Data for 2013 are preliminary. Access data table at: http://www.cdc.gov/nchs/data/databriefs/db162_table.pdf. SOURCE: CDC/NCHS, National Vital Statistics System.

The percentage of children under the age of 18 who live with both biological parents has also significantly decreased during this period of time (Figure 6-2) and the living arrangements of children under 18 with a single parent has increased particularly living with only their mother. While women are specifically and biologically made for motherhood, the culture says they can be all things to all people. And while they can do the things of a father — at least some of them — they can't **BE** a father. The same metaphysical insight is also true for men. They are born biologically and genetically for the role of fatherhood and not motherhood; and while they can do the things of a mother, they can't **BE** a mother. And children, as they grow up, realize these differences even if they don't know how to verbalize it.

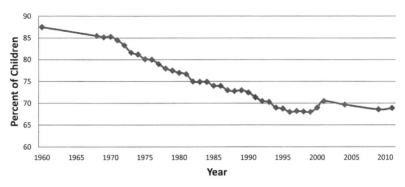

Figure 6-2: Percentage of children under 18 living with both biological parents 1960–2011

So in another extremely problematic statistic is that the percentage of children living only with the mother (Figure 6-3) has grown most prominently in those mothers who have never been married (Figure 6-4). This is detrimental to many of these women and certainly to the children. It has been noted that the "poverty gap" has widened significantly with the increased rate of unintended and non-martial pregnancy in the United States (Figure 6-5). If you start with a group of women who are, to begin with, below the poverty level and look and compare them to the women who are at greater than 200% above the poverty level, there has been an increase in the gap of those women below the poverty level versus those who are not. Since 1994, when the "poverty gap" was at a 2.6 fold difference, by 2006 it increased to a 5.5 fold difference.

Figure 6-3: Living Arrangements of Children Under 18 with One Parent

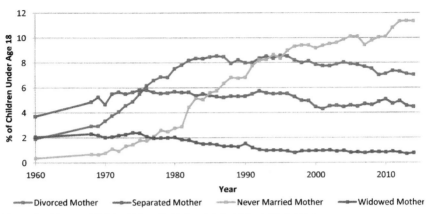

Figure 6-4: Percent of Children Living with Mother Only by Mother's Marital Status

What good is it for women and their children to be left in poverty when in fact there is a solution to that? The solution is to enter into stable relationships. The solution is not to look at men as insemination factories, but look at men as human beings with lives also to be fulfilled and in turn for those men to affirm women as cherished members of humanity that are equal but not the same. One of the major problems of the feminist movement has been that they saw equality in the same light as they would find "sameness." They would often say that men are very promiscuous. We should be able to be. Instead of saying we should try to help men not be so promiscuous and in turn they can help you not to be. There is nothing more magnificent than one spouse who loves the other and vice versa because of who they are because the mother of your children is special in the husband's eyes and in the eyes of God. And the father of your children is special, not only for who he is, but in the eyes of God as well.

With the decrease in the number of marriages, there has been a concomitant increase in the number of couples who are not married but are cohabiting with a member of the opposite sex. This is noted in Figure 6-6 from 1970 through 2010. But there are distinctive problems of cohabiting relationships (when compared to marriage) — Table 6-1.

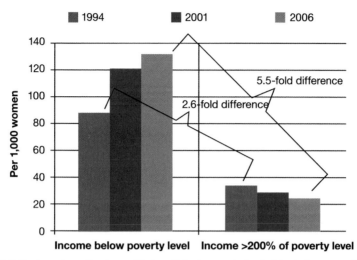

Figure 6-5: The "poverty gap" has been widening with the increased rate of unintended pregnancy in the U.S.

Trends shown here are among women aged 15 to 44 years. Based on data from: Finer LB Zolna MR. Unintended pregnancy in the United States; Incidence and disparities, 2006. Contraception 2011 84(5):478-485

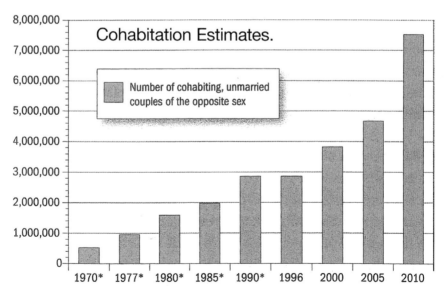

Figure 6-6: Cohabitation. *Census Bureau estimate. Sources: U.S. Census Bureau, Current Population Survey, March and Annual Social and Economic Supplements, 2010 and earlier. Not all of these are in the reproductive age group.

Table 6-1: The distinctive problems of cohabitating relationships (when compared to marriage)

- Odds of recent infidelity increased more than two-fold.
- Increases the net odds of eventual marital infidelity by 39%.
- Rates of separation were 5 times as high.
- Once separated, they are less likely to reconcile.
- Cohabitants reflect a relatively low level of commitment.
- The children suffer from significantly elevated rates of emotional and behavioral disorders.

Treas J, Giesen D: Sexual Infidelity Among Married and Cohabiting Americans.
   Journal of Marriage and the Family 62 (2000): 48–60.
Georgina Binstock and Arland Thornton, "Separations, Reconciliations, and Living Apart in
   Cohabiting and Marital Unions," Journal of Marriage and Family 65 (2003): 432–43.
Scott M. Stanley, Sarah W. Whitton, and Howard J. Markman, "Maybe I Do: Interpersonal Commitments
   and Premarital or Non marital Cohabitation," Journal of Family Issues 25 (2004): 496–519.
Susan L. Brown, "Family Structure and Child Well-Being: The Significance of Parental
   Cohabitation," Journal of Marriage and Family 66 (2004): 351–67.

Some of these problems include the increased rate of recent infidelity once married, the rates of separation are significantly higher and once they are separated, they are less likely to reconcile. In cohabitation, the couples reflect a relatively low level of commitment and the children suffer from significantly elevated rates of emotional and behavioral disorders. This is not a kind portrayal of the cohabitating couple. There is this notion that you don't buy a pair of shoes unless you try them on so why would you marry somebody that you don't know better. The only thing they mean by "better" is whether or not they can have sexual "satisfying" genital intercourse. Ultimately the relationship between husband and wife can be so much more than that if one is willing to learn and enter the depth of the relationship. Cohabitating couples generally are less likely to do that. And even married couples aren't perfect at it, but they haven't had much direction either because the whole sense of the culture over all these many years has been to just let this go on its own and even if the children suffer, we don't care about that. We only care about what the couple wants at a particular moment in time. This is truly a short-sighted view of human relationships.

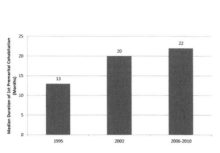

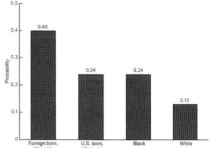

Figure 6-7: Median Duration of 1st Premarital Cohabitation: Women aged 15–44.

SOURCES: CDC/NCHS, National Survey of Family Growth, 2006-2010.

Figure 6-8: Probability of a pregnancy leading to a live birth in the first year of a first premarital cohabitation among women aged 15-44, by Hispanic origin and nativity and race: United States, 2006–2010

National Health Statistics Reports • Number 64 • April 4, 2013

While the median duration of a first premarital cohabitation has increased some in the last 15 years, it still doesn't generally go past 2 years in duration (Figure 6-7), and the probability of a pregnancy leading to a live birth in the *first year* of a first premarital cohabitation is shown for various ethnic groups to range from 13% to 40% (Figure 6-8). What happens with these children?

Table 6-2: Percent of children experiencing at least one transition by age 12 among children of mothers with low education. (Top 10)*

Country	Born to cohabitating couples	Born to married couples
United Kingdom	66	39
United States	41	26
Poland	31	7
Hungary	30	16
Estonia	25	27
France	23	14
Belgium	22	6
Norway	21	15
Netherlands	21	9
Austria	15	10

See http://worldfamilymap.ifstudies.org/2017/
*The difference between the two columns is statistically highly significant (Two sample t-test, p = .015).

In 2017, the World Family Map Report investigated the question of the increase in births to cohabiting couples and its contribution to instability in children's lives. **Data from life histories of individual children born to cohabiting couples in the United States and Europe showed that these children are about twice as likely to see their parents split before they reach age 12** even when controlling for the educational level of mothers and grandmothers. The study also found that family instability is higher in countries where more children were born to cohabiting couples and that growth of cohabitation is associated with increases in the instability of the children's family. Put in other words, **marriage seems to be associated with more family stability for children across much of the globe whereas cohabitation is typically associated with more instability** (see Tables 6-2, 6-3 and 6-4).

Table 6-3: Percent of children experiencing at least one transition by age 12 among children of mothers with moderate education (Top 10)*

Country	Born to cohabiting couples	Born to married couples
United Kingdom	60	31
Lithuania	50	20
United States	45	27
Hungary	35	12
Russia	31	20
Estonia	22	21
Romania	22	6
Norway	21	11
Belgium	20	10
Italy	16	0

See http://worldfamilymap.ifstudies.org/2017/
* The difference between the two columns is statistically highly significant (Two sample t-test, p = .004).

The worst data was generated in the United Kingdom and the United States and is truly a blight on both nations. Not all countries were evaluated for this, but it was truly an international assault.

Table 6-4: Percent of children experiencing at least one transition by age 12 among children of mothers with higher education (Top 10)*

Country	Born to cohabitating couples	Born to married couples
United Kingdom	53	27
United States	49	18
Russia	32	20
Austria	20	8
Estonia	19	14
France	18	9
Norway	17	8
Georgia	10	8
Belgium	8	8
Netherlands	4	6

See http://worldfamilymap.ifstudies.org/2017/
* The difference between the two columns is statistically significant (Two sample t-test, p < .05).
Again, the UK and the US lead the list.

CHAPTER 7:

Preterm Birth

One might wonder why it is that one would want to bring the issue of prematurity into this discussion. Did you know, for example, that prematurity is the leading cause of mental and motor retardation in the United States? You already know that prematurity leads to a very significantly increased risk of infant mortality. What you probably don't know though is that the prematurity rate has increased significantly since the 1960s. But once again, the headline is that there has been a decrease in the prematurity rate (Figure 7-1).

Figure 7-1

U.S. preterm birth rate falls to a 17-year low in 2013

BY LUCAS FRANKI

The U.S. preterm birth rate in 2013 was the lowest since 1996, reaching the Healthy People 2020 goal 7 years early, in a report from the March of Dimes.

Even so, the rate of 11.4% earned only a C on the March of Dimes' report card because it did not meet the organization's goal of a 9.6% rate by 2020. "The U.S. still has one of the highest rates of preterm birth of any high-resource country," Dr. Jennifer L. Howse, March of Dimes president, said in a statement.

The rate was at 12.8% in 2006, but since then it has declined slowly every year. There were more than 540,000 premature babies born in

2006, but fewer than 460,000 in 2013. Overall, about 231,000 fewer babies were born preterm since 2006 through sustained intervention, saving $11.9 billion in health care costs, the March of Dimes noted.

Preliminary data for 2013 show that Vermont had the lowest preterm birth rate at 8.1%, followed by California at 8.8%, and New Hampshire at 9%. At 16.6%, Mississippi had the highest rate; Alabama and Louisiana were at 15.1%. The Southeast United States had the highest preterm birth rates of any region. The five highest rates were in the Deep South, and only Virginia had a rate below 12%. Data are from the National Center for Health Statistics.

lfranki@frontlinemedcom.com

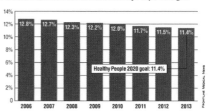

Premature birth rate for 2013 meets Heathy People 2020 goal

Healthy People 2020 goal: 11.4%

2006: 12.8% 2007: 12.7% 2008: 12.3% 2009: 12.2% 2010: 12.0% 2011: 11.7% 2012: 11.5% 2013: 11.4%

Notes: Based on final birth data from the National Center for Health Statistics for all 50 states, the District of Columbia, and Puerto Rico. Figure for 2013 is preliminary.
Source: March of Dimes

The article cited in Figure 7-1, which was published in *OB-GYN News* and circulated for free to most obstetrician-gynecologists and is related to data from the National Center for Health Statistics, seems to indicate that since 2006, there has been a significant decrease in prematurity rates. The graph shown says that it goes from 12.8% down to 11.4%. And yet, if you look at Figure 7-2 which looks at the prematurity rate in the United States from 1967 through 2013, you do see the decline that is noted in Figure 7-1. But what you don't see in that figure is the much lower prematurity rates that were present many years earlier and how they've significantly increased over this period of time.

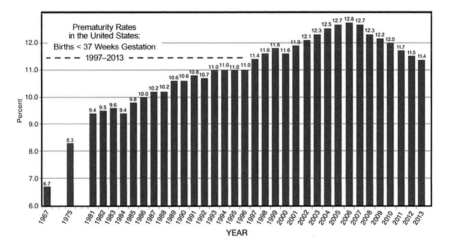

Figure 7-2: Prematurity Rates in the United States: Births <37 Weeks Gestation, 1967–2013

In Figure 7-2, the prematurity rates that are identified for the 17 years in Figure 7-1 are separated with a hashed line across the graph at the point where these can be identified. Before then, the prematurity rate was always lower than what it was in all of the more recent data.

There's data in the medical literature that would suggest that much of prematurity is related to sexually-transmitted diseases of some type. These are not the usual typical ones such as gonorrhea or chlamydia, although that may be the case at times, but it is related to a whole variety of other bacteria that include both aerobic and anaerobic bacteria and can be treated with antibiotics. The prematurity rate at the Pope Paul VI Institute for the last several years is now at 5.4% which is significantly decreased from a comparative population that we've looked at where it was 12.0%. We've developed a Prematurity

Prevention Protocol that actually works and we've talked about it to a number of people, but very few people are interested including maternal fetal medicine specialists. It again raises the question, "Do they really care?" Additionally, the large number of first trimester abortions has also contributed to this increased prematurity rate. It is a **national disgrace** and a **national tragedy!**

We do know that premature babies can do fairly well in the neonatal intensive care unit. We also know that many hospitals like their neonatal intensive care unit to be full because it's one of the highest producing (income producing) sections of the hospital. We also know that we can give fairly good care to premature babies, but we also know that the better place is almost always inside the uterus until full term. So that should be one of our goals and it is a goal that can be accomplished.

CHAPTER 8:

Sexually-Transmitted Diseases (STDs)

With the advent of contraception and abortion, there has been a concurrent increase in the number of people who suffer from sexually-transmitted diseases. Many of these have seen an increase in spite of the use of various types of contraception or "protection." An example of this would be the widespread distribution of condoms by the United States Agency for International Development between 1984 and 2003. This is shown with the concomitant increase in the spread of HIV/AIDS during this same period of time (Figure 8-1). Condom distribution was to prevent AIDS, but actually AIDS increased, so you have to wonder why it is that way? Well, for example, condoms can break. The ability of the small size of the HIV virus (much smaller than a sperm) can likely penetrate some of the condoms. And the biggest problem of all is that, while some of the people who use them buy into the idea that condoms can be protective, they get complacent over time and don't use them and then they can be exposed to the potential for AIDS.

These are problematic and yet understandable complications of the utilization of this type of a contraceptive "protective" technique.

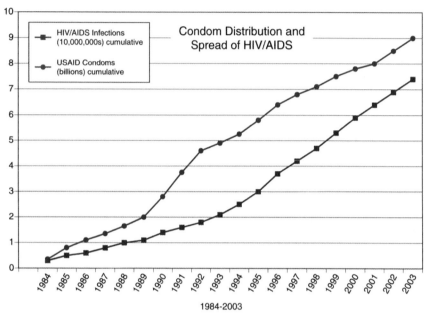

Figure 8-1: The global increase in HIV/AIDS infections compared to the number of condoms distributed abroad by the United States Agency for International Development (USAID) (1984–2003).

Data from the CDCs Mortality Statistics attributable to both men and women is seen in Figures 8-2 and 8-3. Both curves for men and women show an exponential rise with men being much worse than women because it affected men more. On the right hand of each of these graphs, there is the mortality rate from a variety of other types of conditions such as heart disease, stroke, cancer, homicide, diabetes. Over time, the HIV deaths significantly increased. These are real people with real problems and while the AIDS community along with the larger community took this seriously and pitched in to help them with government financing, they've now got this epidemic somewhat under control but at a huge human cost (not financial in the usual sense).

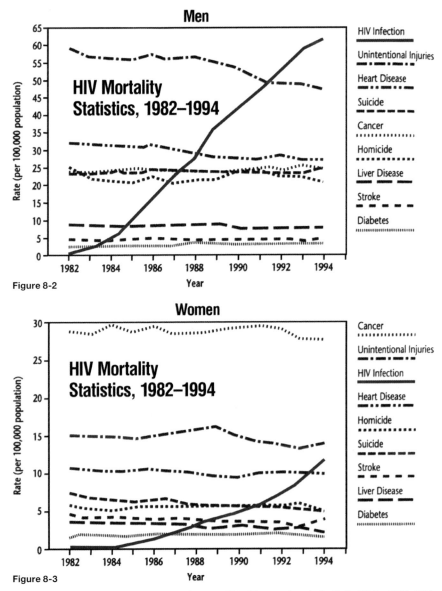

Figure 8-2

Figure 8-3

The leading causes of death among men and women 25 to 44 years of age in the United States 1982–1994. The rising incidence of mortality from HIV infection is shown. From: CDC/mortality statistics attributable to HIV infections among men (Figure 8-2) and women, United States, ages 25–44, MMWR 45:121-125, 1996.

Genital herpes (Figure 8-4) has also increased as well as genital warts. Genital warts is caused by human papilloma virus (HPV) (Figure 8-5). Many thought that if you got vaccinated for HPV, we would see a huge decrease in HPV infections, but it hasn't happened. Herpes infections have also increased. Both of these are sexually transmitted. With herpes, if you deliver the baby vaginally and there is an active herpes lesion, the baby can get a herpes pneumonia and that pneumonia can be devastating to that baby — another part of the "litter" that is strewn on the highway of the sexual revolution.

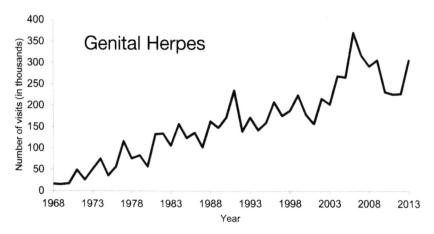

Figure 8-4: Genital Herpes — Initial Visits to Physicians' Offices

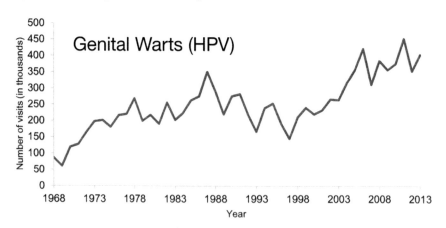

Figure 8-5: Genital Warts (HPV) — Initial Visits to Physicians' Offices

Chlamydia has also increased and to some extent replaced the appearance of gonorrhea (Figure 8-6 and 8-7). Chlamydia can be a sort

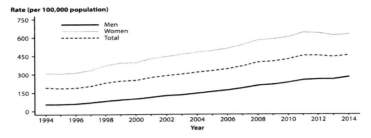

Figure 8-6: Chlamydia — Rates of Reported Cases by Sex, United States, 1994-2014.

NOTE: As of January 2000, all 50 states and the District of Columbia have regulations that require the reporting of chlamydia cases.

of silent disease which leaves the uterus, tubes and ovaries diseased with adhesions (scar tissue) and often does not have symptoms. Gonorrhea can do the same, but it has decreased (Figure 8-8). Now the problem with gonorrhea is that, according to an article in the Washington Post, it suggests that "gonorrhea is becoming an untreatable disease" because the antibiotics used have become resistant (Figure 8-9).

You would sort of think that the incidence of something like Chlamydia would not be a big problem in a relatively conservative, mid-west city such as Omaha, Nebraska. And yet, in Figure 8-7 the Chlamydia rate in Douglas County which is basically Omaha, Nebraska, has increased significantly as shown.

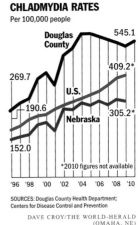

Figure 8-7

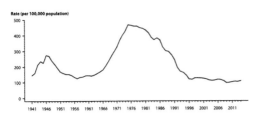

Figure 8-8: Gonorrhea — Rates of Reported Cases by Year, United States, 1941–2014

ANTIBIOTIC RESISTANCE

Gonorrhea risks 'becoming an untreatable disease'

THE WASHINGTON POST

Dame Sally Davies, Britain's chief medical officer, has reportedly written to doctors and pharmacies in Britain sounding the alarm on antibiotic resistant

centers' highest ranking for antibiotic resistance, classifying it as an "urgent threat." At that time, the CDC reported that around a third of cases were resistant to at least one antibiotic.

Figure 8-9: From Washington Post, Dec. 2015

With the AIDS epidemic under some level of control, an epidemic of syphilis has been significantly increasing particularly in men who have sex with men (Figure 8-10). Syphilis is a destructive disease, it can

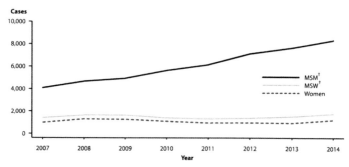

Figure 8-10: Primary and Secondary Syphilis — Reported Cases by Sex and Sexual Behavior, 27 Areas*, 2007–2014. *27 states reported sex of partner data for ≥70% of reported cases of primary and secondary syphilis for each year during 2007–2014. 1MSM = men who have sex with men; MSW = men who have sex with women only

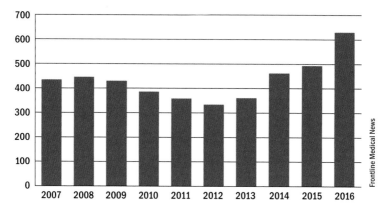

Figure 8-11: Increasing incidence of congenital syphilis. From: OB. Gyn. News: Syphilis Spike — Prenatal care is critical, 52:6, November 2017. Note: Based on data from "Sexually Transmitted Disease Surveillance 2016." Source: Centers for Disease Control and Prevention.

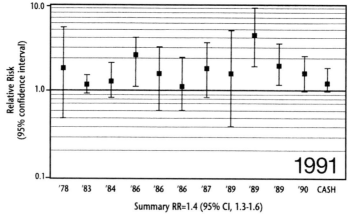

Figure 8-12: Breast Cancer and the birth control pill (1991). The relative risk of breast cancer in women under the age of 45 with long-term use of oral contraceptives: A summary of the results of 12 case-controlled studies[1].

be very painful and problematic. Congenital syphilis has been on the increase again (Figure 8-11). It is almost as if syphilis is replacing HIV.

You wouldn't normally think of breast cancer as being a sexually-transmitted disease and yet the relationship of breast cancer and the use of oral contraceptives has been well known since the late 1980s and early 1990s (Figure 8-12). And yet, only recently in the *OB-GYN News* for September 2014, does it say, "Recent use of OCs linked to breast cancer risk" (Figure 8-14). A significant rise in the number of cases of Stage I breast cancer is also not new data (Figure 8-13). It was supplied by the National Cancer Institute and it is indeed related chronologically to the pathophysiologic effects of the birth control pill. Many people want to know why is breast cancer so prominent.

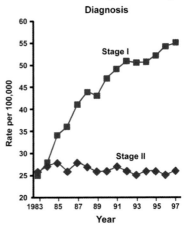

Figure 8-13: This graph shows the increasing rate of Stage I breast cancer. The diagnosis of Stage I breast cancer increased 113 percent between 1983 and 1997 (Data from: Surveillance, Epidemiology and End Results-SEER-Program of the National Cancer Institute).

Well, fundamentally, that is the likely reason. It's a very problematic development which most in the medical profession realize is happening, but they're not willing to do anything about it. This is, indeed, tragic.

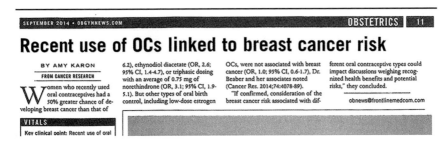

SEPTEMBER 2014 • OBGYNNEWS.COM
OBSTETRICS 11

Recent use of OCs linked to breast cancer risk

BY AMY KARON
FROM CANCER RESEARCH

Women who recently used oral contraceptives had a 50% greater chance of developing breast cancer than that of 6.2), ethynodiol diacetate (OR, 2.6; 95% CI, 1.4-4.7), or triphasic dosing with an average of 0.75 mg of norethindrone (OR, 3.1; 95% CI, 1.9-5.1). But other types of oral birth control, including low-dose estrogen

OCs, were not associated with breast cancer (OR, 1.0; 95% CI, 0.6-1.7), Dr. Beaber and her associates noted (Cancer Res. 2014;74:4078-89).

"If confirmed, consideration of the breast cancer risk associated with dif-

ferent oral contraceptive types could impact discussions weighing recognized health benefits and potential risks," they concluded.

obnews@frontlinemedcom.com

VITALS
Key clinical point: Recent use of oral

Figure 8-14: OB-GYN News, September 2014

There's also been an increase in cervical cancer in patients who use oral contraceptives. This is probably due, to a great extent, to the human papilloma virus through promiscuous sexual contact (Figure 8-15).

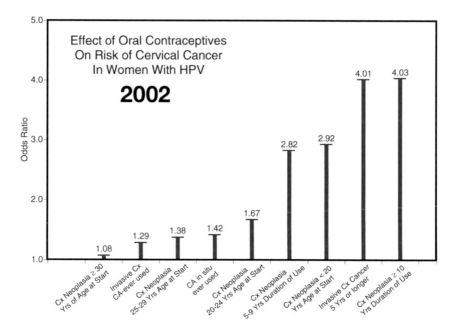

Figure 8-17: Cervical Cancer. The effect of oral contraceptives on the risk of cervical neoplasia and cervical cancer in women with human papilloma virus, expressed in odds ratios.[3]

CHAPTER 9:

Drugs, Crime, Suicide

Since the 1960s, there has also been an increase in the use and abuse of various drugs and along with it, an increase in crime rates and suicides. The rates for new cocaine users in the ages 12 to 17 have increased significantly from 1965 through 1998 (Figure 9-1).

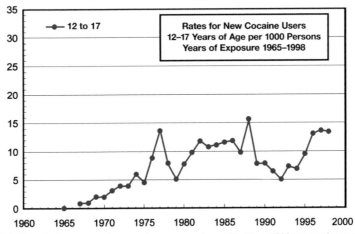

Figure 9-1: The rates for new cocaine users in young people age 12–17 per 1000 persons by year of exposure, 1965–1998.[19]

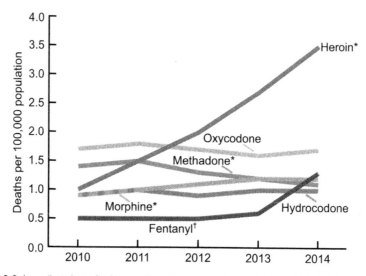

Figure 9-2: Age-adjusted rates for drug overdose deaths involving selected opioids: United States, 2010–2014

*Increasing or decreasing trend is statistically significant. † Increase from 2013 to 2014 is statistically significant. NOTES: Drug overdose deaths are identified using underlying cause-of-death codes X40—X44, X60—X64, X85, and Y10—Y14. Deaths may involve other drugs in addition to the referent drug (i.e., the one listed). Deaths involving more than one drug (e.g., a death involving both heroin and cocaine) are counted in both totals. Caution should be used when comparing numbers across years. The reporting of at least one specific drug in the literal text improved, from 67% of drug overdose deaths in 2010 to 78% of drug overdose deaths in 2014. SOURCE: NCHS, National Vital Statistics System, Mortality files linked with death certificate.

More recently, the increase in the use of heroin and fentanyl (a newer synthetic and very strong opiate), have really increased significantly and they are impacting a large number of people (Figure 9-2). Violent crime rates have also increased significantly since 1960. While again, there has been noted some decrease since the mid-1990s, it's still significantly higher than it was back in the early 1960s (Figure 9-3). Juveniles taken into police custody who were referred to a criminal or adult court from 1972 to 2014 is noted (Figure 9-4). It has definitely increased and the suicide rate amongst teenagers (Figure 9-5) has also increased. This increase has been much worse for young men than it has been for young women, but in either case, it's a real tragedy.

While racial disparities always exist in medicine and diseases, they're not always the same racial disparity. In Figure 9-6, you see the age-adjusted drug overdose death rates which show a significantly higher rate for non-Hispanic white persons, and much lower rates for non-Hispanic black and Hispanics. In addition, middle-aged white mortality has skyrocketed, especially amongst men and women who

Figure 9-3: Violent Crime Rates, 1960–2010

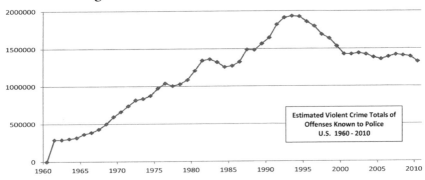

Figure 9-3: The estimated violent crime rate of offenses known to police, in the United States from 1960–2010. Updated Source: http://www.ucrdatatool.gov/Search/Crime/State/RunCrimeTrendsInOneVar.cfm

Figure 9-4: Percent of juveniles taken into police custody referred to criminal or adult court from 1972 to 2014

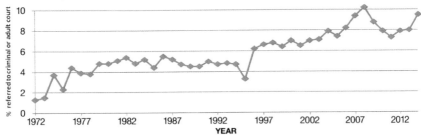

Citation, U.S. Department of Justice, Federal Bureau of Investigation. (2010). Sourcebook of criminal justice statistics: Percent distribution of juveniles taken into police custody. Retrieved from website: http://www.albany.edu/sourcebook/pdf/t4262010.pdf. U.S. Department of Justice, Federal Bureau of Investigation. (2015). Table 68: Police disposition of juvenile offenders taken into custody, 2005. Retrieved from website: https://www.fbi.gov/about-us/cjis/ucr/crime-in-the-u.s

Figure 9-5: Suicide Rate (per 100,000 Persons in Age Group) for Persons 15–19 Years of Age

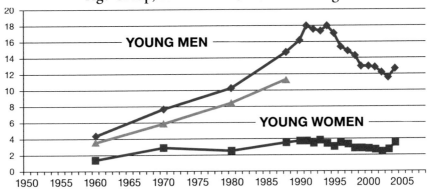

have a high school diploma or less. Those with a 4-year college degree or more show it has increased a little, but not as much (Figure 9-7) and life expectancy has decreased (Figure 9-8).

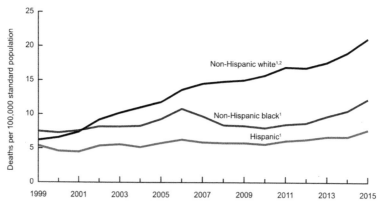

Figure 9-6: Age-adjusted drug overdose death rates, by race and ethnicity: United States, 1999–2015

[1]Significant increasing trend, p < 0.005. [2]Rate for non-Hispanic white persons was significantly higher than for non-Hispanic black and Hispanic persons, p < 0.001. NOTES: Deaths are classified using the International Classification of Diseases, Tenth Revision. Drug overdose deaths are identified using underlying cause-of-death codes X40- X44, X60-X64, X85, and Y10- Y14. Deaths for Hispanic persons may be underreported by about 5%. Access data table for Figure 3 at: https://www. cdc.gov/nchs/data/databriefs/db273 _ table.pdf#3. SOURCE: NCHS, National Vital Statistics System, Mortality.

Figure 9-7

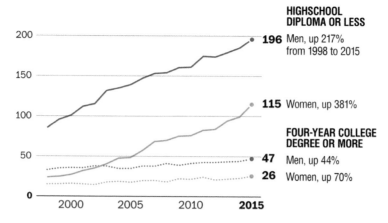

MIDDLE-AGED WHITE MORTALITY HAS SKYROCKETED

Overdose, suicide and alcohol-related deaths per 100,000 for white non-Hispanics ages 50 to 54, by gender and education (from Washington Post)

HIGHSCHOOL DIPLOMA OR LESS
196 Men, up 217% from 1998 to 2015
115 Women, up 381%

FOUR-YEAR COLLEGE DEGREE OR MORE
47 Men, up 44%
26 Women, up 70%

Source: "Mortality and morbidity in the 21st century," Anne Case, Angus Deaton, Princeton University.

THE WASHINGTON POST

Figure 9-8: USA Today, December 21, 2017

NEWS

U.S. life expectancy drops for second year

Reports cite opioid abuse among reasons for decline

Kim Painter
Special for USA TODAY

Health researchers have some grim news for Americans: We are dying younger, and life expectancy is down for the second straight year — something not seen in more than half a century.

One culprit is the opioid epidemic, which cuts down young adults at alarming and increasing rates, the researchers said.

The numbers are "disturbing," said Robert Anderson of the National Center for Health Statistics. The branch is part of the Centers for Disease Control and Prevention, which released two reports Thursday. One focused on all causes of

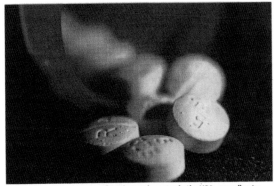

Opioid abuse kills young people at increasing rates in the USA, according to research from the Centers for Disease Control and Prevention. PATRICK SISON/AP

CHAPTER 10:

Sexuality Issues

I began this discussion with the entrance of a more widespread use of sexually-explicit materials that also gained some level of social acceptance with the efforts of Hugh Hefner. However, it has continued to grow and expand in ways that many could never have imagined. Pornographic material is available on many television sets in the home based on cable television and certain channels that seem to prey on people with their pornography. That's not to say anything about the internet which is even worse. The internet is loaded with pornographic material within the reach of anybody who wants to type in the address and perhaps pay a few dollars. Some of the addictive component of pornography are itemized in Table 10-1.

Table 10-1: Pornography

- 1955 — expansion of sexually explicit material
- Now, 40,000,000 U.S. adults regularly visit porn websites.
- In Christian homes 47% say it is a problem in their home.
- 9 in 10 children between the ages of 8 and 16 have viewed porn on the Internet.
- Pornography is addicting
- And it affects marriage.

As an odd sort of association to this, the Nebraska Department of Correctional Services recently issued a ban on all pornographic magazines, books and drawings effective in January 2017 (Figure 10-1). By now, you're probably asking the question why do they have pornography in the prison? That's a very legitimate question and one that has an answer. Apparently there have been some inmate protests in other states and lawsuits over First Amendment rights that seem to always be the fall-back position. So it's problematic that the government would be feeding these people sexually-explicit material which doesn't help anything. Do they have a First Amendment right to it? There are certain organizations in this country who think everybody has a certain right to anything notwithstanding the harm that it may do to the individual, the family or the broader community. That comes down to a question of **freedom and responsibility**. More on that later.

EFFECTIVE JAN. 8

Prison system to ban pornography

BY PAUL HAMMEL
WORLD-HERALD BUREAU

Nebraska's Frakes says use promotes 'hostile work environment'

LINCOLN — Nebraska prison inmates soon will have fewer choices of reading materials.

The Nebraska Department of Correctional Services has issued a ban on all pornographic magazines, books and drawings effective in January, joining a growing number of states that have issued such blanket restrictions.

In some states, the restrictions have prompted inmate protests and lawsuits over First Amendment rights.

But the move was cheered by family-oriented groups in Nebraska, as well as a nationally known prison consultant from Colorado.

Gene Atherton, who also is a former prison warden, said a growing number of states are adopting bans on pornography to curtail sexual misconduct by inmates and protect staff, particularly women, from seeing such materials or becoming the object of sexual fantasies.

"I have no First Amendment sympathies for inmates who think they have a right to their pornography," Atherton said.

The pornography ban was announced in a memo to inmates last week.

In the memo, State Corrections Director Scott Frakes

See Pornography: Page 2

Figure 10-1: From Omaha World-Herald, Omaha, Neb., 2017.

As an obstetrician-gynecologist I've been involved in academic medicine now for almost 50 years, and this may sound strange, but only until recently, I'd never heard of the term "transgender." So I was interested in a survey that was published in 2014 the data for which came from the 2013 National Health Interview Survey (NHIS). The data for this is shown in Tables 10-2 and 10-3. There were 231,697 people interviewed and equally divided between men and women. There are some very interesting results in this.

	% men	% women
Straight	96.7	96.6
Gay/Lesbian	1.8	1.4
Bisexual	0.4	0.9
Refused	0.5	0.6
I don't know the answer	0.4	0.4
Something else	0.2	0.2

Total: N = 231,697

Table 10-2: Sexual orientation among adults ages 18 and over by sex: United States 2013[1] Sexual orientation in the 2013 National Health Interview Survey (NHIS): a quality assessment vital health statistics 2(169). 2014 (CDC). (Total n = 231,967).

- The term transgender was not one of the initial responses. In a **follow-up response** to the answer "something else" **5.4 percent** responded as **Transgender**.

- There were 400 respondents that said they were "something else"

- 400 x .054 = 21.6 of **231,967** were identified as transgender.

Table 10-3: In the NHIS survey for 2013

First of all, the term transgender was not asked of any of these people. They were asked if they were gay or lesbian and 1.4% of the women and 1.8% of the men said yes (that's less than 2% of the population). Less than 1% said that they were bisexual; about ½ of 1% refused to answer the question; 0.4% of those questioned did not know the answer. A final answer was given which was "something else." And 0.2% of women and 0.2% of men answered that in the affirmative.

So in the NHIS survey for 2013, they followed up those who responded to the question of sexual orientation as "something else." There were 400 respondents out of 231,697 who said they were "something else." And, when followed up, 5.4% of those 400 reported they were transgender. This is a total of 21.6 out of 231,697 who identified themselves as transgender. And yet, in our current culture, based especially on the mass media, the term transgender has become part of our language and yet we don't even know what it is, but it represents apparently a very small percentage of people.

In addition to that, we know that homosexuality is conveyed on television programs — especially sitcoms, and in other programs — as if it is a very common problem and that if someone were to guess, they would probably say 25-50% of people were homosexual. At least it seems that way given how they are represented in all of these areas. And yet, less than 2% of the population is actually, by their own admission, homosexual. So why is it that the mass media and the producers of these television programs emphasize participation by people who are publicly gay? If your answer was because they wanted to represent the reality of gay and lesbian identity, then your answer would be wrong because only 1 in 50 identify as such. If your answer is that people tune in because of their apparently insatiable desire to hear and look at people who are gay for whatever reason, and that it improves ratings which in turn improves the ability of the program to make money, then you're probably on the right track. In any regard, it has caused a considerable amount of confusion in the culture and this confusion continues with the whole issue of "gender identity" which is something nobody ever heard of before a few years ago.

Table 10-4: Gender Identity

- Male
- Female
- Other
  - Facebook put together a list of gender identities as defined by Urban Dictionary. There were over 50 gender options.
  - Facebook collaborated with its network of support, a group of LGBT advocacy organizations to determine this list.

In gender identity (Table 10-4), people are generally identified as either male or female but Facebook put together a list of gender identifies as defined by Urban Dictionary and there were over 50 gender options. To come up with these gender options, Facebook collaborated with its network of support, a group of LGBT advocacy organizations to determine this list. In other words, there's no science behind these gender identification terms. There's been no medical person, psychologist or others who've actually done realistic research for this sort of thing to put clarity into it. Again, it's just being done in order to increase the revenue being generated by these different groups. But at the same time, it's also creating an enormous level of misunderstanding while at the same time, promoting a significant ignorance.

CHAPTER 11:

The Family, Women and Children Under Attack

Marriage over many generations and millennia has meant the public commitment of one man to one woman for their lifetime. This was often put into practice by various religious groups who had a very significant contribution to make relative to the religious notion of permanence and commitment. The state, in turn, passed laws supporting and administrating this bond. At the same time, outside of this, there were things such as polygamy which had a little bit of a religious backing in some groups, but not in the overwhelming majority of groups and was made illegal. But in today's world, we have same-sex marriage, cohabitation and something called sologamy. In sologamy, you could marry yourself, and apparently there are kits that you can

Table 11-1: Marriage under attack

• Marriage — male to female	• Cohabitation
• Same-sex marriage	• Sologamy — marrying yourself

Figure 11-1: The Domino Effect of Trends that Endanger Women, Children and Families (1955–2004)

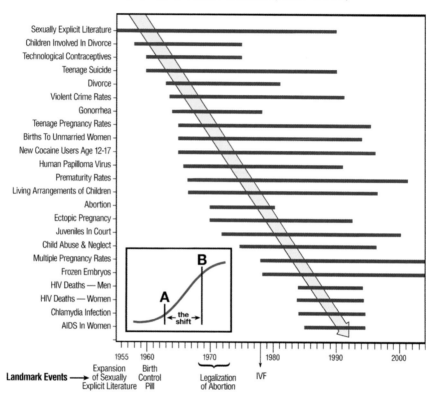

order to do that. I actually don't have one of those kits and have never seen one, but I've heard about them. But with all of the gender identity questions, the question of transgenderism, the questions of all the options of gender identity, the overplayed issue of homosexuality, etc., etc., and now with its impact on marriage, there's a huge impact on the family which is really what this is all about. And, to a great extent, it's generated by an agnostic or atheistic approach — or a situational ethics approach — a philosophy of relativism which is antagonistic to Judeo-Christian values. This book isn't meant to try to dissuade people from whatever their religious belief might be, but it is here to at least ask for tolerance of people who think differently than you might. One of the big problems with the left-leaning culture that has developed is that they all think they're absolutely correct and nobody who thinks differently could possibly be correct. So the only thing we can do is get rid of them — get rid of the institutions, get rid of the churches, get rid of whatever it might be.

Through this analysis, however, we now know that there is an impact of one thing to the next and to the next and to the next. It's like a domino effect of a series of trends that endanger women, children and families. This is shown in Figure 11-1 with the graph of "The Shift" identified, the horizontal blue lines represent the beginning and the end of that shift if it actually ends in the scope of this particular graph. When it does end, it ends at a much higher rate than when it started.

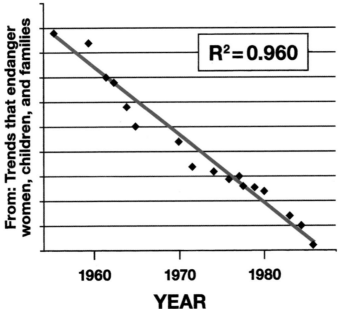

Figure 11-2: Each measured at the beginning of the exponential rise (see Figure 11-1)

Figure 11-2: A regression line establishing a significant linear relationship beginning with point A of the shift. An R^2 value of 0.960 reveals a statistically highly consistent linear relationship.

In Figure 11-2, a **linear regression line** has been drawn statistically from the beginning of each of these trends. The R^2 (the correlation coefficient) equals 0.960 which is **statistically highly significant.** In other words, there appears to be a highly significant correlation between the trend that has developed starting with the appearance of sexually-explicit literature followed by technological contraception and the great impact that it had on abortion, IVF, etc. Clearly some of these are more major than others, but abortion has been devastating, the birth control pill through all of its sexually-transmitted diseases, breast cancer, cervical cancer, etc., has been devastating — along with the many other things that have impacted the family. And, it seems to continue to go forward. It seems to continue to get worse; and, as I have noticed, nobody wants to get to the bottom of this.

I've also noticed that in the United States with something called "freedom," there is this overall attitude and approach to problem-solving that you only solve the problem once the problem has occurred as opposed to looking ahead or downstream, to see whether or not somebody could foretell that these events would occur. Was there nobody who could do this?

Indeed, there was and he was roundly criticized. His name was Pope Paul VI, he is now Blessed Pope Paul VI, soon to be canonized, and he was the author during his pontificate of a papal encyclical (letter) called *Humanae Vitae.* I know that those of you who might be interested in science are now wondering why are we talking about religious things and why are we talking about *Humanae Vitae.* There is a reason for this and the reason is that Pope Paul VI laid down clearly what he thought would happen once artificial contraception and its allied "friends" were brought to the world. What he predicted was not anywhere so detailed as what I have presented here. And yet the generalities of what he predicted are seen in what is presented here.

Many theologians dissented from Pope Paul VI's papal encyclical, and one of the criticisms was that he made predictions that he could not back up. His predictions had no sound sociological or cultural evidence to them. They said basically that there was no evidence that these things would occur; which, incidentally connects with what I had just written that in the United States particularly, we have this attitude that a problem does not exist unless it exists.

The idea of insight appears to be nonexistent except that if the person who disagrees with the insight and has their own insight, then their insight is correct. It's a very self-absorbed kind of idea relative to freedom. Ultimately, it is freedom without responsibility or with irresponsibility.

If you go back to the use of hormonal contraception and this issue of depression among adolescent women, in a study published in 2016, those on oral contraceptives or progestin-only birth control pills are 1.8 to 2.2 times at higher risk for developing depression. This is not a new idea. This has been around and shown over many decades, but nobody pays attention to it. Mothers want their daughters on contraception so that they don't get pregnant. And yet birth rates amongst young women who are not married are 9 times greater (45%) compared to 1960 when it was only 5%. The doctor doesn't know how to treat anything in that age group unless they put them on birth control pills. (Here I'm referring to symptoms of a woman's reproductive system).

Table 11-2: Depression among adolescent women associated with hormonal contraception

Method	Relative Risk
Non-Users (Control Group)	1.00
Combined Oral Contraceptives	1.8
Progestin Only BCP	2.2

From: Skovlund CW, Morch LS, Kessing LV, Lidegaard: Association of hormonal contraception with depression. JAMA Psychiatry 73 (11): 1154-62, 2016.

So in all of this, we have worked on the development of something we call the **Family Distress Index (FDI)**. In Figure 11-3, the FDI is presented from the years 1960 to 2015 (Est). **As the number in this graph increases, the distress within the family is worse.** This Family Distress Index is made up of the divorce ratio, non-marital childbearing data, prematurity rate, abortion and suicide rate in teenagers. It's plotted on a 5-year basis and it's our hope that we can continue to develop this FDI and publish it every 5 years so these changes can be monitored.

Figure 11-3

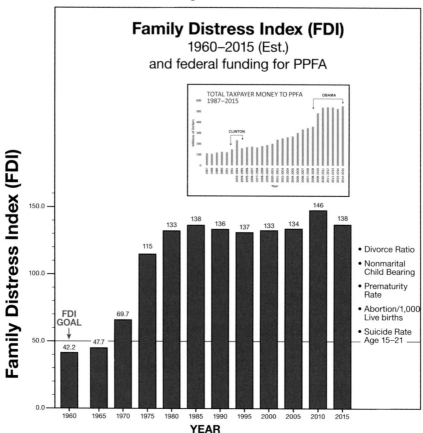

This chart was produced by the Pope Paul VI Institute, ©2017

In Figure 11-3, we have the FDI graphed and timed with the tax-payer funding of Planned Parenthood. And so, we can also develop what we would call a goal of the Family Distress Index and that is identified with the red line running horizontally across it at about 50.0. This would be a very low rate and while some would say that I'm interested in pushing everybody back into the 60s and 50s, that's not the case. On the level of this data, it is the case, but we don't have to go back to the 1950s for all of the other things that maybe weren't so good at that time. We think that we've improved the state of things and yet we really haven't. We've actually made it worse.

As a result of this type of an analysis, we now know that the cultural trends that have occurred over these last 60 years, while they're often referred to as "progressive," are, in fact, starkly **"regressive." The Planned Parenthood cultural mantra has been a failure! The results of the work of Planned Parenthood has been one big experiment without informed consent.** Our politicians have gone for it because they think this has got to be good. All of our problems seem to revolve around sex and childbearing. And yet, they've been made worse. There's no arguing that the Planned Parenthood mantra of "Every Child a Wanted Child" has blown up in its face. I've never seen so many so-called "wanted children" who are so unloved. It's such a tragedy and it has had a huge impact on people everywhere.

People can deny this, they can rationalize against it, they can be critical of the analysis or the way I have presented it, they can do all sorts of things with this and I certainly will understand that, but in so doing, **they have their head in the sand** and they have to get their head out of the sand; they have to look around; they have to see what is there.

CHAPTER 12

Who gets hurt the most? Men or women?

It appears that what has happened over the last 50 to 60 years in the United States (and perhaps elsewhere) is that the road that has been traveled following the lead of the "sexual revolution" promoted by Hugh Hefner and his "sex without love" dogma, and the "sex without kids" dogma of Helen Gurley Brown also left in its wake a road that is littered with the victims of this "revolution." These victims are larger in number than we probably ever could have imagined. But this book suggests, in an epidemiological way, that the move has not been nearly so liberating as promoted; and that, in fact, it may have enslaved people — its victims — in ways that likely could have been predicted at the time, but because of what appears to be a significant insensitivity to these types of outcomes (the entire movement is immersed in self-absorption), we now know that millions of people have been damaged and hurt.

Men and women have both been hurt — in some cases irrevocably so. But a question that can and should be asked is who has been hurt most? Men or women? One can start with the over 60 million abortions that have been performed in the United States which includes, of course, aborting little human babies that are both female and male. One might not be able to see clearly any other issue that has been so strikingly violent and destructive as abortion. Keep in mind that abortion was promoted initially as an approach to solve social problems, relationship and economic issues. But medicine and surgery are not solutions to these types of problems, and in fact, they may make the problems worse. These procedures are fundamentally **puritan in scope** sweeping the real issues "under the carpet" making it so much more difficult to resolve.

Keep in mind that women are the ones who have been physically aborted through a surgical procedure referred to as induced abortion. They're the ones who suffer the consequences of subsequent preterm births for example, or perforation of the uterus with hemorrhage at the time of the procedure, or even as we're now learning, an increased risk of maternal mortality. For men, it would seem to be that they get off "scot free!" And yet there are undercurrents of a destructive movement such as this one that lead to what Eunice Kennedy Shriver called "The Hard Society." Our hearts have become cold!

In the midst of a lot of discussion about being more sensitive, being more caring, being more this, more that, we're not even close to improving these. When people talk about the polarization that exists within the United States, **the polarization exists from the inconsistent and violent way in which human life is handled and disvalued.** If our children in the womb are so worthless that they can be wiped out with the stroke of a curette, then what's that mean to the woman who is being aborted; a woman who is carrying this child, her natural right to be a part of the nourishment and nurturing of her small child (her offspring). For this to happen that woman needs to be socially aborted before she's reached the medical or surgical abortionist. As an obstetrician-gynecologist for many years, I've often wondered if it isn't because, as a culture, we're very afraid of women. We're afraid to try to be of help in some ways. We're afraid of being direct and honest for fear that there can be some angry retaliation (premenstrual symptoms) and we don't know what to do with that. Indeed some women (and men) have been scarred by previous rejections. The men often have a form of hormone dysfunction (andropause). Both of these conditions can today be easily evaluated and successfully treated.

Ultimately, if one can challenge the circumstances, offer a helping hand and communicate that you really do actually care for her in a realistic sense, then it opens up a whole different perspective for relationships. This applies to the friendship and real love between spouses. When we as a culture say that we are highly polarized, a good deal of that culture started when the Supreme Court of the United States changed the abortion picture to one that is horrifyingly violent, extraordinarily detached and ultimately very uncaring for that woman and, of course, for her baby. If the culture cannot accept this child, it is a direct rejection of its mother. So women are horribly hurt by all of this whether or not they even see it in self-reflection.

What about the extraordinary increase in sexually-transmitted diseases that clearly, at least on the surface, affect women more than men? Conditions such as Chlamydia, syphilis, cervical cancer, tumors of the liver, increased risk of heart disease, blood clotting and yes, even breast cancer. If you read closely the medical literature, you will see that we have a profession that has changed from taking care of the individual patient to not being concerned about the individual patient, but rather more concerned about a population of people. So when you ask your doctor about whether birth control pills are associated with breast cancer, they say, well not really because the overall percentage of women who get cancer of the breast related to the birth control pill is actually very small. If you have a field full of 100,000 women, that number is small. But if that woman is in your office and looking for solutions to regular everyday problems such as family planning issues, if the physician gives her birth control pills he/she is acting as an accessory to the development of her breast cancer.

There are other issues such as an increase in divorce, long-term and short-term after-effects of cohabitation, the overwhelming additional responsibility for a woman to be the main caretaker for their children without any spousal assistance and, in particular, not having a loving and reasonable male role model in the family; the pain and hurt that comes with divorce, especially for the children within the family. This number literally is in the millions and millions of people.

Cultural shift in antagonism to men

- Something ominous is happening to men
- Everyone knows this but rarely speaks about it.
- "Men don't need help," they say.
- 1 in 5 boys are diagnosed with hyperactivity disorder (this is at a much higher rate than in young girls).
- millions of children raised in families without fathers
- poorer grades in school
- young men's wages are decreased 20% from 1977 to 2010
- Men "don't show up on time."
- Women "go to better colleges."
- Suicide rate is increased
- 2 times more likely to overdose on drugs
- 73% of overdose deaths in New Hampshire were men
- 77% of suicides were men — 43% increased over a 5-year period of time disproportionately in men
- greater than 90% incarcerations are men
- females graduate from high school at a higher rate than young men
- women go to college at a higher rate than young men
- women more than men go to graduate school, law school and medical school
- fewer men get married than they used to
- women's wages have increased
- men are described as being "privileged"
- women "more oppressed"
- men die five years younger than women
- commentators on television referring to "toxic masculinity" because of their natural assertiveness and competitiveness

If you look at the male labor force participation rate, it has decreased significantly since 1970 for all ethnic backgrounds (Figure 12-1) and the median household income for married-parent families with at-home mother in 2010 dollars from 1949 to 2010 is shown in Figure 12-2. There has been little meaningful growth in the purchasing power of these incomes.

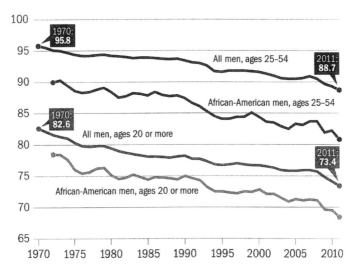

Figure 12-1: Declining Male Labor-Force Participation Rates, Percent of the Civilian Population. Source: Current Population Survey, U.S. Bureau of Labor Statistics.

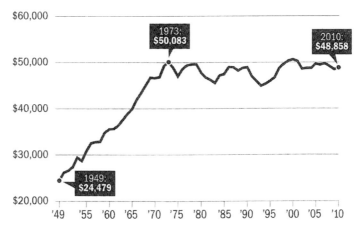

Figure 12-2: Median Household Income, Married-Parent Families with At-Home Mother in 2010 Dollars, 1949-2010. Source: U.S. Census Bureau, Current Population Survey, Annual Social and Economic Supplements.

So, if we look, as we have in this book, at the upward spiral of conditions that have actually never been seen at such a high frequency in our culture before, having started with the betrayal of women with physically oriented pornography, then expounding upon philosophical approaches that seem right, except they're not. They are rationalizations for "what appear to be good reasons but are not real reasons."

Now we have infertility, millions more abortions because of

discarded embryos in IVF, but worse, that it never deals with the diseases that these women actually have as a cause of their infertility or their miscarriages. How can we say that we are caring for the healthcare of women when we don't even look for the underlying cause of these issues; and then, of course, we don't treat whatever those issues might be? About 75% of women who have infertility have endometriosis and another 15% or so will have polycystic ovaries; both of which are real medical conditions often associated with pelvic pain, irregular cycles, irregular bleeding, even the long-term effect of having cancer of the uterus or breast. If these conditions are treated, one can get rid of the pelvic pain, the severe menstrual cramps, the long-term risk of these conditions, while at the same time improving their fertility.

I remember listening to one of the women in the United States Senate when healthcare legislation was being put forward that, "These women must have their contraception. It is part of their healthcare needs." But don't they understand? Don't they realize that birth control pills don't treat anything. In fact, they create their own physician-induced diseases that oftentimes the woman would not get if she were not on these birth control pills. So who is hurt most? Well, it may not be the man or the woman that's hurt most, but perhaps the child, either preborn or early in their life after birth when their family is disintegrating around them. You wonder why there is this great polarization in the United States and probably in many areas of the world. We have lied to each other with regard to so many of these issues and there's the old saying that if one is lied to enough, that lie becomes, at least to them, their view of truth.

So on the cover of this book we have a physician along with a young couple, both of whom have **blinders** on. It's a highly destructive type of relationship. So we do have a lot of work to do ahead of us to set all of this into the right direction; and it will not be easy because we have so much "self-protection" being exhibited in these debates. If one wants to eliminate the polarization, one needs to learn how to give of oneself to another not, as is so often done, take for oneself whatever is in the way so that "sex without love" and "sex without kids" can rule the day. But then, they go down a path in their life where they never experience love and, while children should be viewed as the "supreme gift of marriage," they are, in many ways, the innocent bystanders of a horribly prejudicial and discriminatory society where the parents are easily willing to hurt them, physically, emotionally and, I think, spiritually. Our culture has been searching in its own inept way for sexual meaning. But they appear to have been looking in all the wrong places.

Is this really the best we have to offer?

CHAPTER 13:

The Public Health Crisis

Public health can be defined as the art or science of protecting and improving community health by means of preventive medicine, health education, control of communicable diseases and the application of the social and sanitary sciences. It becomes a crisis when it becomes a "turning point" moving especially in the direction of significantly weakening health. The data that has been compiled for this book points to the **critical nature** of these health and sociological events.

There is, however, another component to this which makes it so much more difficult and complex. **It is also a crisis in values** — those things that are important to us. I don't refer here to monetary things as would usually be the case, but rather things that significantly alter human relationships for the worse. It also involves questions about the role of the medical profession in the ongoing cultivation of this public health crisis and the recognition that **a revolution of values** which stimulates a growth in new approaches and new ideas that are aimed at reconnecting science, medicine, sociology, spirituality and other approaches with **substantive values** that are proven to be connected to the resolution of these difficulties. The entire culture, ultimately, needs to be participating in this.

In this book, I have looked at multiple issues for both sociological and public health trends from data that has overwhelmingly come from national data collection systems run through the Center for Disease Control, the National Center for Vital Statistics, medical journals, newspaper reports, while putting them in a chronologic order to see how one ultimately connects with the other. Ultimately, it challenges the paradigm of Hugh Hefner which says the "sexual revolution" that he proposed has "no victims." Rather than based on substantive facts, it was pushed through imaginary hope. But as a surgeon, I recognize that, "hope is not a strategy!" With the advent of contraception on a widespread basis, and then abortion and then *in vitro* fertilization (none of which ever get to the root cause of the underlying problems), there is a cascading series of events that has occurred that are all one connected to the other. Many would say that this is a faith-based approach and while it is true that faith may play a role in how some people reach these conclusions, ultimately **these conclusions can be reached by reason**. Reason is a capability of the intellect that is ultimately shared by all of humanity and, I might add, only by humanity! Thus there exists the capability of reaching an overall collegial, community decision.

Table 13-1: Trends Involving the Endangerment of Women: 1955-2017

Physical Endangerment	Emotional Endangerment
• Breast cancer	• All physical endangerments
• Cervical cancer	• Divorce
• Contraception	• Teenage suicide
• Human Papilloma Virus (HPV)	• Teenage pregnancy
• Abortion	• Abortion
• Ectopic pregnancy	• Child mistreatment and neglect
• Multiple pregnancy	• Prematurity
• HIV/AIDS	• Low birth weight infants
• Chlamydia	• Fatherless families
• Intimate partner violence (IPV)	

The trends that involve the endangerment of women is a list that is very long and that list is presented in Table 13-1. It is not likely to be a complete list, but it is certainly an adequate list to begin the discussion on this public health crisis. These have all been reviewed in this book and the data presented reveal that this is literally epidemic at this point in time.

There has been an ongoing debate in medicine since the early 1990s as to whether or not oral contraceptives increase the risk of breast cancer. On December 7, 2017, the *New England Journal of Medicine* published an article entitled, "Contemporary Hormonal Contraception and the Risk of Breast Cancer." Their conclusion was, "The risk of breast cancer was higher among women who currently or recently used contemporary hormonal contraceptives than among women who had never used hormonal contraceptives, and this risk increased with longer durations of use; however, the absolute increases in risk were small." But if you were one of the women who got breast cancer because of the use of oral contraceptives, the impact on that woman is not "small."

There have also been identified trends involving the endangerment of children (see Table 13-2). These also involve physical as well as emotional endangerment. These are listed and have been covered in more detail throughout this analysis. The trends involving the endangerment of families are also physical and emotional and are listed in Table 13-3. Many on these three lists affect women, children **and** families. They also have an impact on men and they have a sociological and economic impact on the family overall. In fact, male wage earners have decreased their productivity over the last 30 or 40 years. In many cases, they have lost meaning in their lives. What was once criticized as a too paternalistic culture is quickly becoming a maternalistic culture which also has the potential to become out of balance. So these are all issues that need further examination connected with a set of values that are truly meaningful for everyone.

In the previous chapter, we showed a cascading series of events that reveal a significant increase in the event in a time-recorded sequence that basically started in the mid-1950s, the flames of which were fanned with the advent of widespread technological contraception which then led to abortion and then to *in vitro* fertilization. What so many people don't really understand is that none of these have been therapeutic (technological contraception, abortion or IVF). In fact, the oral contraceptive is a medication that is used for a variety of different medical issues that young reproductive-age women have, but it doesn't treat any of those conditions. It only suppresses the symptoms to a certain degree and once the birth control pill is discontinued, the symptoms tend to return. With abortion, we have for a long time now tried to solve sociological issues and relationships with a distinct form of medical violence, which on its surface would almost guarantee that no resolution would come. With *in vitro* fertilization, we have an approach for the treatment of infertility which doesn't even look for the underlying causes. Thus, it cannot treat any of the underlying causes and the woman who comes into an IVF doctor's office with these diseases will also leave that office with those same diseases with a relatively small chance of becoming pregnant which is also very expensive and unaffordable by many.

TABLE 13-2: Trends Involving the Endangerment of Children: 1955–2017

Physical Endangerment	Emotional Endangerment
• Teenage suicide	• All physical endangerment
• Violent crime	• Divorce
• HPV	• Depression (suicide)
• Prematurity	• Teenage pregnancy
• Low birth weight	• Unmarried mothers
• Abortion	• Living arrangements
• Cocaine use	• Abortion
• Juveniles in court	• Child mistreatment and neglect
• Child abuse and neglect	• Absent fathers
• Multiple pregnancy	
• Chlamydia	

TABLE 13-3: Trends Involving the Endangerment of Families: 1955–2017

Physical Endangerment	Emotional Endangerment
• Divorce	• Living arrangement of children
• Children affected by divorce	• Abortion
• Teenage suicide	• Juveniles in court
• Teenage drug use	• Child mistreatment and neglect
• Premature birth	• Sexually explicit literature
• Low birth weight	• Absent fathers

Indeed, we could relatively easily speculate that a nation that exhibits such disrespect for human relationships and for the integrity and dignity of the human person and such a poor sense of freedom cannot survive. This public health crisis, it could be argued, is the single greatest challenge for the future of this great nation. It literally eats at the very core of the family... at its very heart! **It would appear that our hearts have turned cold!**

CHAPTER 14:

Is There Hope?

Yes, there is hope! In some ways, it's not real easy to find, but it is there. But we need to take the blinders off (Figure 14-1). Let's take a look at a few things.

Figure 14-1: The Blinders must come off.

In our textbook on **NaProTECHNOLOGY** we have shown that you can reduce the prematurity rate by a significant margin and we can reduce the multiple pregnancy rate by 10 fold in patients who have infertility. We've also shown and we have more data to come which will reveal that the per-woman pregnancy rates in a **NaProTECH-NOLOGY**-driven program of infertility evaluation and treatment is higher than it is with the IVF programs. Ultimately, it's also less expensive. There are a whole variety of other conditions that can also be treated such as recurrent ovarian cysts, premenstrual tension syndrome, premenstrual dysphoric disorder, abnormal bleeding without hysterectomy, etc.

The maternal mortality rate in Ireland, for example, when abortion was illegal, was 4.0 in 2009, but in the United Kingdom where abortion was legal in 2009, it was 9.4 or greater than 2 times as high. The infant mortality rate in Ireland for the same year was 3.2 vs. the United Kingdom which was 4.7 (Table 14-1).

Table 14-1: Maternal and infant mortality rate where abortion is illegal (Ireland) compared to where abortion is legal (United Kingdom)

	Year	Maternal Mortality	Infant Mortality
Ireland (illegal)	2009	4.0	3.2
United Kingdom (legal)	2009	9.4	4.7

As cited in: Lanfranchi A, Gentles I, Ring-Cassidy E: Complications: Abortion's Impact on Women, deVeber Institute for Bioethics and Social Research, Toronto, 2013

The infant mortality rate in Poland in 1990 when abortion had just become illegal was 16, but as it remained illegal, it went down to 8 and 6 by 2008. Along with that, the deaths from cerebral palsy in Poland also decreased significantly after abortion was made illegal (Table 14-2 and Figure 14-2).

Table 14-2:
Infant Mortality Rate per 1,000 births — Poland

	Abortion Legality	Infant Mortality Rate
1990	Just Made Illegal	16
2000	Illegal	8
2008	Illegal	6

As cited in: Lanfranchi A, Gentles I, Ring-Cassidy E: Complications: Abortion's Impact
on Women, deVeber Institute for Bioethics and Social Research, Toronto, 2013

Figure 14-2

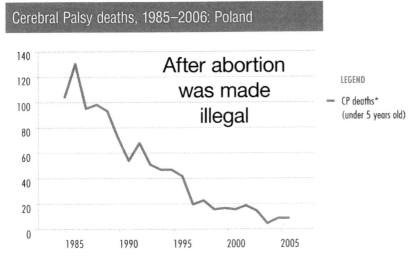

Source, Cerebral Palsy deathsi n Poland, 1985–2006, Poland Central Statistical Office.

In a study that was published in 2003, the majority of sexually-active teens wished they had waited longer before beginning sexual activity. This was higher in young girls than it was in young boys, but they were both above 50% (Table 14-3).

Table 14-3: The majority of sexually active teens wish they had waited longer before beginning sexual activity[1]

Wish They Had Waited Longer Before Starting Sexual Activity	All sexually Active Teens	Sexually Active Boys	Sexually Active Girls
YES	63%	55%	72%
NO	32%	39%	25%

Source: National Campaign to Prevent Teen Pregnancy, June 2000. NOTE: Survey covers sexually active teens age 12-17. Cited in: A Report of the Heritage Center for Data Analysis. Recker RE, Johnson KA, Noyes LR: Sexually Active Teenagers are More Likely to be Depressed and to Attempt Suicide. The Heritage Foundation, June 2, 2003.

Other data seems to support that, particularly with regard to value formation. If you compare the use of alcohol with sexual activity, those who do not drink had a much lower rate of sexual activity than those who had been drinking recently (Figure 14-3). And furthermore, the

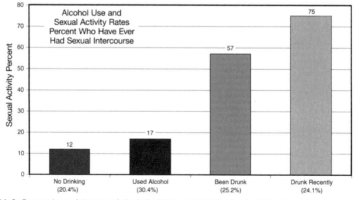

Figure 14-3: Comparison of the use of alcohol with sexual activity rates(p<.001, chi-square analysis).[1]

relationship between sexual values and sexual activity rates related to the question, "It is against my values for me to have sex when I am an unmarried teen" went from a very low rate of 7.8% of those who strongly agreed with that statement, to 72.4% for those who strongly disagreed with it (Figure 14-4).

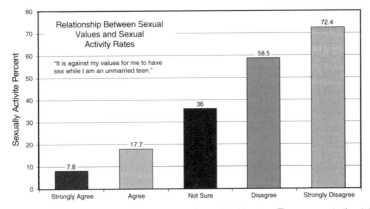

Figure 14-4: The relationship between sexual values and sexual activity rates. The response to the statement. "It is against my values for me to have sex while I am an unmarried teen" compared to involvement in sexual activity. Based on a survey of 1537 students, 15 to 17 years old.[1]

Recently, there was a study published relative to the odds of divorce in 1,397 Catholic women who never used NFP (natural family planning) compared with 105 Catholic women who ever used NFP. The percentage of couples who got divorced and had never used NFP was higher than it was for NFP users or who had used NFP. For a long time, people in the natural family planning movement argued this question in the same way, but there was limited data available. This data is still somewhat limited and it's not perfect, but the very values that respect fertility as something that's normal and healthy are the same values that promote ultimately good relationships.

Odds of divorce in 1,397 Catholic Women who never used NFP compared with 105 Catholic Women who ever used NFP.

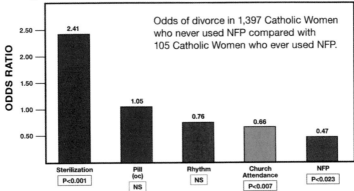

Figure 14-5: Adapted from: Fehring R: Divorce Rates in women who ever used NFP. Analysis of NSFG Data 2006-2010. Linacre Quarterly, 81:190-194, 2014.

Is there hope?

- In the United Kingdom when abortion was legal, the increase in maternal mortality from childbirth was 235% higher than in Ireland where it was illegal.
- The infant mortality rate in the United Kingdom under legal abortion was over 140% higher than in Ireland when abortion was illegal.
- The infant mortality rate in Poland after abortion was made illegal decreased over 260%.
- The number of deaths from cerebral palsy in children less than 5 years of age decreased 7.5-fold in Poland.
- The majority of sexually-active teens wished they had waited longer before beginning sexual activity.

Figure 14-6: The 1244-page medical textbook that describes NaProTechnology®. (Pope Paul VI Institute Press, Omaha, NE, 2004). A second edition is in preparation.

- There is an inverse relationship between the use of alcohol and sexual activity rates. As the use of alcohol increases, so does sexual activity increase.
- As the use of alcohol decreases, the sexual activity rate also decreases.
- When the value to have sex while you are an unmarried teen is strongly agreed to, the sexual activity rate is the lowest.

- When the teenager strongly disagrees with that value, the sexual activity rate increases by over 900%.
- Preliminary evidence suggests that the ever use of a natural method of family planning carries with it a statistically significant decrease in the divorce rate.
- There are prematurity prevention protocols that have decreased the incidence of prematurity to below 6%.
- Conditions such as premenstrual syndrome, premenstrual dysphoric disorder, and recurrent ovarian cysts have been shown to be adequately treated.
- The "per-woman" pregnancy rates are higher when the cause of the infertility problem is identified and adequately treated.

CHAPTER 15:

Freedom and Responsibility: The Real Revolution Needs to Begin

In the United States of America we live in a nation that has been proud of its ability to establish and support a people who are free. Indeed, to a certain extent, that pride and capability is true and to be respected. However, the last 50 to 60 years has given birth to a distorted view of freedom that is ever growing larger. This distorted view will destroy us if we do not revise and change this approach.

We have developed a notion of freedom that basically says that, "We can do anything we want to do as long as it's not illegal." Over the years, the law has protected liberty but in the last 50 to 60 years it has contributed in a major way to the domino effect of our culture in disarray and decline. It has divested a sense of responsibility from the concept of freedom and one can seriously question if freedom in the absence of being responsible is actually freedom at all.

In fact, one could suggest that when a person acts in ways that are irresponsible under the guise of freedom or liberty that it can be a form of enslavement; almost a tyrannical state of existence controlled by the so-called "cultural norms." This is very serious and it requires very serious considerations.

If two people are "friends" the question can legitimately be asked, "Would either friend do harm to the other on purpose?" The answer to that should be without any difficulty a resounding **NO!** A friend is a person that one knows, likes and trusts. A friend is a person who does not wish harm to the other. In this regard, one can also develop a concept of "sexual friendship." This is placing one's sexual thoughts and ideas into the context of not wishing harm to the other person or, for that matter, any other person. In this regard, too, one can develop a list of the "freedoms of sexual friendship." (Table 15-1).

Table 15-1: Freedoms of Sexual Friendship:

- The freedom from unwanted pregnancy
- The freedom from multiple complications of contraception, including its downstream complications
- The freedom from venereal diseases and their bad effects
- The freedom from the complications of abortion
- The freedom from the sorrow that descends upon the family when an unmarried daughter becomes pregnant
- The freedom to explore brained-centered rather than genital-centered sexuality

- The true freedom to embrace both love and life.

1. Adapted from: Hilgers TW: The Pregnant Adolescent: A Challenge to the Community. Int Rev Nat Fam Plan, 343-358: 1977.

This list of freedoms to each individual comes out of the value of doing no harm to another. So you have the freedoms from unwanted pregnancy, the multiple complications of contraception including its downstream complications from venereal diseases and their bad effects, from the complications of abortion, from the sorrow that descends upon the family when an unmarried daughter becomes pregnant and ultimately the freedom to explore a brain-centered rather than a genital-centered sexuality.

This requires a significant paradigm shift within the culture. It is not hard to recognize that this may, in fact, be somewhat difficult.

And yet, the crisis that we face is so significant that it is time that we begin developing an approach that allows these freedoms to come into existence.

A Hefner approach to sexuality is really a hedonistic approach and one which is focused completely on pleasure in the absence of any concern for the other. The ones who have the largest vulnerability in this are men because they are so vulnerable to external influences. Before long, one adapts a new form of behavior thinking that it is good and correct. Ultimately, this is a rationalization (rationalization is the use of "what appears to be good reasons" for "real reasons.") and in the area of sexuality, they are living in their own never-never land.

This will also require the development of some level of self-mastery of genital stimulation. This type of self-mastery is not a denial of the pleasure that one can obtain through this but the realism that there are other significant non-genital rewards in this level of friendship that will ultimately take place as a result. Furthermore, it allows us to discover that there is significant meaning to the sexual relationship beyond pleasure and it is important to the development of a true friendship.

These rewards affect both men and women in a culture where men currently are played as fools (that's another book). Women ultimately are disrespected; their ability to be a life-nurturer is significantly distorted and because of the many actions of men that have been hurtful to women, the culture has accepted the idea that women can carry on without men. Life can be created without human sexual interaction. We can go about our culture **not wanting life** with the apparent thought that it can be turned off at will and turned on again by naively adopting an attitude of wanting life.

The medical profession has led the way in all of this taking on the idea that nothing can be done, so we might as well contracept, sterilize, refer or do abortions and refer or do *in vitro* fertilization (all of which are ultimately destructive and in more or lesser degrees violent). One wonders why do those things in the culture exist and happen? If life and lives are taken so superficially and in many ways selfishly, can there really be no other result or impact. **Ultimately, it is the violent and destructive, downstream impact that contraception, abortion and IVF within the context of the Hefner sexuality concepts that has fractured the good that can come from healthy relationships, healthy treatment of women, healthy approaches to avoiding pregnancy and**

healthy approaches to achieving pregnancy. If you are one of those people who would like to see a change in the culture, then you need to look seriously at these questions and become a part of the solution and not continue as a part of the problem.

Sue Ellen Browder, a former writer for Cosmopolitan magazine in the days of Helen Gurley Brown, noted that Brown's message to the single woman was "hard work and sex will set you free (as long as you don't have children)." Helen Gurley Brown did not see a lack of education or economic opportunity, but rather motherhood as "the insurmountable obstacle to real liberation for women." Gurley Brown claimed that what held women back from success in the corporation was the "built-in mechanism in their bodies that allows them to have babies."

Browder continued that "if you trusted yourself to Helen's lifestyle teachings (as many young women did and still do), you'd soon come to believe the way for a smart woman to be free and to succeed in her career and her life was to (1) Work hard; (2) Take the pill or use some other contraceptive; and (3) If the contraceptive failed, get an abortion. In an unseen way, which eluded me (Browder) at the time, the sexual revolution was both *for* unmarried sex and *against* motherhood. The two went hand in hand.

She goes on to say that "the Cosmo Girl was not a real person but a *persona,* a mask of the single girl, lonely and alone in the world, that she could put on to turn herself into the object of a man's sexual fantasies. In *Sex and the Single Girl,* Helen Gurley Brown wrote: "When a man thinks of a single woman, he pictures her alone in her apartment, smooth legs sheathed in pink silk capri pants, lying tantalizingly among dozens of satin cushions, trying to read but not very successfully, for he is in the room, filling her thoughts, her dreams, her life." And as a journalist for Cosmopolitan, she noted that there was also the childless "Cosmo Girl" who encouraged the reader to exchange their authentic identity for this unreality. Where is the lonely single woman to let go of her "guilt" (moral concerns) and sleep with any man she pleases, even if he was married.

In the beginning, Browder wrote "there was no Cosmo Girl, or at least as far as I could tell, there weren't many real-life copies of her yet. She was mostly a product of Helen's clever imagination, a marketing fairy tale. Yet, we wrote about this sexually 'free' woman as if she really existed. Over time, readers who regarded the fantasy as real began to live out the Cosmo lifestyle. Within a decade or so, those of us who wrote regularly for the magazine, began to find single women openly sleeping with their boyfriends everywhere, and I no longer had to make up so many anecdotes to produce an article Helen deemed publishable. Between 1970 and 1999, the percentage of unmarried couples just living together increased more than six fold. Such is the power of skillfully crafted propaganda to change people's attitudes and lives. **Fiction had become a reality. And literature had become fake.** The fantasy of a woman as a radical individualist who belongs only to herself and is disconnected from others — betrayed the truth of women's lives — and this was the **Cosmo** girl all created initially by literary soldiers (writers) 'for hire.'" And Hefner's Playboys now had a partner. Love and life had been disconnected! The world was shown that love without life and life without love, the "new" paradigm, was absent any value or meaning.

As a culture, we seem in some ways to be searching for sexual meaning, but in doing so, we have abandoned and rejected the real substance of the sexual encounter. This encounter is not just physical, but is also spiritual, physical, intellectual, creative, and communicative and psychological and emotional (**SPICE**). **The SPICE encounter can be 24 hours per day, 7 days a week, instead of 3-4 times per week. For the last 50 to 60 years, we have been looking in all the wrong places. It will happen once we fully embrace both love and life!**

As we have looked at so many problems and difficulties that exist in our culture, we can see how so many of them revolve around the values that we have held important or those that we have discarded. If this is going to be corrected, it will be accomplished only with the rejection of some of the new "values" we have supported over these years. This will not be easy, but what we have now is also not easy. The culture and the medical profession, especially those who take care of reproductive age women, must look at the direct downstream impact of the treatment of fertility as if it were a disease or of looking at pregnancy as the "number two venereal disease." Fertility is a part of health and one of the values we need to take a hold of is the value of making healthy decisions and stop abusing our fertility and our sexuality. It will occur if we can become involved in a real revolution — **a Revolution of Values needs to begin now!**

Limited Glossary

Abortifacient:
Capable of producing abortion. Usually used in the context of early abortion before, at or shortly after the time of implantation.

Estrogen:
A hormone produced from the ovaries during the course of a woman's ovulation cycle. It is also produced in large amounts in pregnancy.

Hedonism:
Behavior based in the belief that pleasure is the most important thing in life.

Nathanson, Dr. Bernard:
Dr. Nathanson was an original member of the National Association for the Repeal of Abortion Laws (NARAL), was himself an abortionist, but discontinued performing abortions once he learned more about the lives that he was destroying. He was an obstetrician-gynecologist.

Ovarian Hyperstimulation Syndrome (OHSS):
This refers to a condition where the ovaries are over-stimulated by medications when a reproductive endocrinologist "superovulates" the ovaries with usually injectable medications. It can be a very serious complication and also can cause death.

Progesterone: A hormone produced in the ovaries following ovulation and is also produced in large quantities during pregnancy.

Puritanism: An approach to problem solving which is camouflaged in strict approaches to morality, but, in reality, does very little to solve underlying problems.

Relativism: A philosophical approach that sees truth in relation to the group or individual that proposes it. The important feature of relativism is that it sees no moral absolutes. Furthermore, it is not based in an objective judgment of what is morally right or wrong. An action might be considered morally wrong today, but through a subjective assessment, it might be considered morally right tomorrow.

Thromboembolism, Venous: This is a situation where a blood clot has formed in a deep vein and then breaks away from the wall of the vein and it circulates up towards the heart and lungs where it can become lodged. It can be a very serious complication and can even lead to death.

Thrombosis: This is a blood clot that forms in the deep veins usually in the legs or the pelvis. It is usually related to some trauma to those veins or to certain medications.

Utilitarianism: The ethical theory proposed by Jeremy Bentham and John Stuart Mill that all moral, social or political actions should be directed toward achieving the greatest good for the greatest number of people without any moral absolutes.

ABOUT THE AUTHOR

Thomas W. Hilgers, MD

Director of the **Pope Paul VI Institute for the Study of Human Reproduction** in Omaha, Nebraska. He began his first research in human fertility in 1968 as a senior medical student. Working at St. Louis University and Creighton University Schools of Medicine, he and his co-workers developed the **CREIGHTON MODEL Fertility-Care™ System**. Those intrinsically involved in the development of this system for the last 41 years, along with Dr. Hilgers are: K. Diane Daly, RN, CFCE; Susan K. Hilgers, BA, CFCE, and Ann M. Prebil, RN, BSN, CFCE (1946–2017).

Dr. Hilgers is currently a Senior Medical Consultant in Obstetrics, Gynecology, Reproductive Medicine and Surgery at the Pope Paul VI Institute and is a Clinical Professor in the Department of Obstetrics & Gynecology at Creighton University School of Medicine. He is Director of the Institute's Academic Programs and its National Center for Procreative Health. He is board certified in obstetrics, and gynecology, gynecologic laser surgery and is a member of the Society of Reproductive Surgeons and the Society of Procreative Surgeons. Furthermore, he is certified by the American Academy of FertilityCare Professionals (AAFCP) as a **FertilityCare™** Medical Consultant (CFCMC). In 1994, Dr. Hilgers, along with his wife, Susan, were named by Pope John Paul II to a 5-year term to the Pontifical Council for the Family and he was also appointed an active charter member of the Pontifical Academy for Life (1994–2017).

He is the author of over 234 professional books, book chapters, poster sessions, articles, videotapes and he has given countless numbers of professional presentations. He has also been the recipient of 16 special recognition awards and 7 research awards. He also directs the largest annual CME program at Creighton University School of Medicine (132 hours per year). He is the recipient of 3 honorary doctorates and was named the Physician of the Year by the Nebraska Family Council in 1997.

Acknowledgements

The author would like to thank Terri Green for her transcription of the manuscript and Matt Johnson for his graphic expertise and layout. Some of the basic research was done with the assistance of our summer research assistance program.

Bibliography

The following are a list of bibliographic references that were consulted in the research to produce this book. Exact citations are generally present with each table and figure cited.

Abma J, Chandra A, Mosher W, et al. "Fertility, Family Planning and Women's Health: New Data from the 1995 National Survey of Family Growth." *U.S. Department of Health and Human Services. Center for Disease Control and Prevention, 1997.*

Abma J, Chandra A, Mosher W, Peterson L, Piccinio L. (1997) Fertility, Family Planning, and Women's Health: New Data from the 1997 National Survey of Family Growth. National Center for Health Statistics. Center for Disease Control and Prevention. Vital and Health Statistics 23(19). Accessed on June 17, 2016 from CDC Website: http://www.cdc.gov/nchs/data/series/sr_23/sr23_019.pdf

Advanced Fertility Center of Chicago. Single Cycle IVF Cost Details, 2017, Retrieved on June 26, 2018 from https://www.advancedfertility.com/ivf-price.htm

American Society of Reproductive Medicine. White Paper: Access to Care Summit. September 2015. Accessed on June 26, 2018 from https://www.asrm.org/globalassets/asrm/asrm-content/news-and-publications/news-and-research/press-releases-and-bulletins/pdf/atcwhitepaper.pdf

Baby Center. Fertility treatment: Your options at a glance, 1997, Retrieved on June 26, 2018 from http://www.babycenter.com/0_fertility-treatment-your-options-at-a-glance_1228997.bc?page=2#articlesection3

Bogaert AF, Turkovich DA, Hafer CL. "A Content Analysis of Playboy Centerfolds from 1953 through 1990. Changes in Explicitness, Objectification and Models Age." *J Sex Res*, 30:135-139, 1993.

Bramlett MD, Radel LF. Adverse family experiences among children in nonparental care, 2011-2012. National health statistics reports; no 74. Hyattsville, MD: National Center for Health Statistics. 2014.

Brind J, Condly SJ, Mosor SW, et al Issues in Law and Medicine, 30:129-140, 2015.

Browder SE. "Subverted: How I Helped the Sexual Revolution Hijack the Women's Movement." *Ignatius Press,* San Francisco, 2015.

California Cryobank. Pricing. January 2018. Retrieved on June 26, 2018 from http://www.cryobank.com/services/pricing/

Cates W, Grimes PA, Smith JC: Abortion as a Treatment for Unwanted Pregnancy: the Number Two Sexually Transmitted "Disease." Presented at: 14th Annual Scientific Meeting, Association of Planned Parenthood Physicians. Miami Beach, FL. November 11, 1976.

Cava M. What Happened When I Visited the Playboy Mansion. *USA Today,* 29 Sept. 2017, p. D1.

Centers for Disease Control and Prevention. "Assisted Reproductive Technology Success Rates, 1995-1999."

Centers for Disease Control and Prevention, American Society for Reproductive Medicine, Society for Assisted Reproductive Technology. *1997 Assisted Reproductive Technology Success Rates: National Summary Report.* Atlanta: U.S. Dept of Health and Human Services; 1999.

Centers for Disease Control and Prevention, American Society for Reproductive Medicine, Society for Assisted Reproductive Technology. *1998 Assisted Reproductive Technology Success Rates: National Summary Report.* Atlanta: U.S. Dept of Health and Human Services; 2000.

Centers for Disease Control and Prevention, American Society for Reproductive Medicine, Society for Assisted Reproductive Technology. *1999 Assisted Reproductive Technology Success Rates: National Summary Report.* Atlanta: U.S. Dept of Health and Human Services; 2001.

Centers for Disease Control and Prevention, American Society for Reproductive Medicine, Society for Assisted Reproductive Technology. *2000 Assisted Reproductive Technology Success Rates: National Summary Report.* Atlanta: U.S. Dept of Health and Human Services; 2002.

Centers for Disease Control and Prevention, American Society for Reproductive Medicine, Society for Assisted Reproductive Technology. *2001 Assisted Reproductive Technology Success Rates: National Summary Report.* Atlanta: U.S. Dept of Health and Human Services; 2003.

Centers for Disease Control and Prevention, American Society for Reproductive Medicine, Society for Assisted Reproductive Technology. *2002 Assisted Reproductive Technology Success Rates: National Summary Report.* Atlanta: U.S. Dept of Health and Human Services; 2004.

Centers for Disease Control and Prevention, American Society for Reproductive Medicine, Society for Assisted Reproductive Technology. *2003 Assisted Reproductive Technology Success Rates: National Summary Report.* Atlanta: U.S. Dept of Health and Human Services; 2005.

Centers for Disease Control and Prevention, American Society for Reproductive Medicine, Society for Assisted Reproductive Technology. *2004 Assisted Reproductive Technology Success Rates: National Summary Report.* Atlanta: U.S. Dept of Health and Human Services; 2006.

Centers for Disease Control and Prevention, American Society for Reproductive Medicine, Society for Assisted Reproductive Technology. *2005 Assisted Reproductive Technology Success Rates: National Summary and Fertility Clinic Reports.* Atlanta: U.S. Dept of Health and Human Services; 2007.

Centers for Disease Control and Prevention, American Society for Reproductive Medicine, Society for Assisted Reproductive Technology. *2006 Assisted Reproductive Technology Success Rates: National Summary and Fertility Clinic Reports.* Atlanta: U.S. Dept of Health and Human Services; 2008.

Centers for Disease Control and Prevention, American Society for Reproductive Medicine, Society for Assisted Reproductive Technology. *2007 Assisted Reproductive Technology Success Rates: National Summary and Fertility Clinic Reports.* Atlanta: U.S. Dept of Health and Human Services; 2009.

Centers for Disease Control and Prevention, American Society for Reproductive Medicine, Society for Assisted Reproductive Technology. *2008 Assisted Reproductive Technology Success Rates: National Summary and Fertility Clinic Reports.* Atlanta: U.S. Dept of Health and Human Services; 2010.

Centers for Disease Control and Prevention, American Society for Reproductive Medicine, Society for Assisted Reproductive Technology. *2009 Assisted Reproductive Technology Success Rates: National Summary and Fertility Clinic Reports.* Atlanta (GA): U.S. Dept of Health and Human Services; 2011.

Centers for Disease Control and Prevention, American Society for Reproductive Medicine, Society for Assisted Reproductive Technology. *2010 Assisted Reproductive Technology Fertility Clinic Success Rates Report.* Atlanta (GA): U.S. Dept of Health and Human Services; 2012.

Centers for Disease Control and Prevention, American Society for Reproductive Medicine, Society for Assisted Reproductive Technology. *2010 Assisted Reproductive Technology National Summary Report.* Atlanta (GA): U.S. Dept of Health and Human Services; 2012.

Centers for Disease Control and Prevention, American Society for Reproductive Medicine, Society for Assisted Reproductive Technology. *2011 Assisted Reproductive Technology Fertility Clinic Success Rates Report.* Atlanta (GA): U.S. Dept of Health and Human Services; 2013.

Centers for Disease Control and Prevention, American Society for Reproductive Medicine, Society for Assisted Reproductive Technology. *2011 Assisted Reproductive Technology National Summary Report.* Atlanta (GA): U.S. Dept of Health and Human Services; 2013.

Centers for Disease Control and Prevention, American Society for Reproductive Medicine, Society for Assisted Reproductive Technology. *2012 Assisted Reproductive Technology Fertility Clinic Success Rates Report.* Atlanta (GA): U.S. Dept of Health and Human Services; 2014.

Centers for Disease Control and Prevention, American Society for Reproductive Medicine, Society for Assisted Reproductive Technology. *2012 Assisted Reproductive Technology National Summary Report.* Atlanta (GA): U.S. Dept of Health and Human Services; 2014.

Centers for Disease Control and Prevention, American Society for Reproductive Medicine, Society for Assisted Reproductive Technology. *2013 Assisted Reproductive Technology Fertility Clinic Success Rates Report.* Atlanta (GA): U.S. Dept of Health and Human Services; 2015.

Centers for Disease Control and Prevention, American Society for Reproductive Medicine, Society for Assisted Reproductive Technology. *2013 Assisted Reproductive Technology National Summary Report.* Atlanta (GA): U.S. Dept of Health and Human Services; 2015.

Centers for Disease Control and Prevention. Estimated HIV incidence among adults and adolescents in the United States, 2007-2010. HIV Surveillance Supplemental Report 2012;17(No. 4). http://www.cdc.gov/hiv/topics/surveillance/resources/reports/#supplemental. Published December 2012.

Centers for Disease Control and Prevention. Monitoring selected national HIV prevention and care objectives by using HIV surveillance data—United States and 6 dependent areas—2013. HIV Surveillance Supplemental Report 2015; 20(No. 1). Available at: http://www.cdc.govo/hiv/library/reports/surveillance/. Published July 2015.

Centers for Disease Control and Prevention. "Mortality Attributable to HIV Infection Among Persons Aged 25-44 Years — United States 1994." *MMWR,* 45:121-125, 1996.

Centers for Disease Control and Prevention, National Center for Health Statistics. (2015). National marriage and divorce rate trends. Retrieved from CDC website on June 15, 2016: http://www.cdc.gov/nchs/nvss/marriage_divorce_tables.htm

Centers for Disease Control and Prevention, National Center for Health Statistics. (2013). "The number and rate of nonmarital childbearing declined from the 2008 peak." Retrieved from CDC: http://www.cdc.gov/nchs/data/databriefs/db162_table.pdf

Centers for Disease Control and Prevention, National Center for HIV/AIDS, Viral hepatitis, STD, and TB Prevention. (2015) Reported Cases of STDs on the Rise in the U.S. Retrieved from the CDC Website: http://www.cdc.gov/nchhstp

Centers for Disease control and Prevention. Sexually Transmitted Disease Surveillance 2004. Atlanta: U.S. Department of Health and Human Services; 2005.

Centers for Disease control and Prevention. Sexually Transmitted Disease Surveillance 2009. Atlanta: U.S. Department of Health and Human Services; 2010.

Centers for Disease Control and Prevention, (2011). *2010 sexually transmitted diseases surveillance. Table 1. Cases of sexually transmitted diseases reported by state health departments and rates per 100,000 population, United States, 1941-2010.* Retrieved from website: http://www.cdc.gov/std/stats10/tables/1.htm

Centers for Disease Control and Prevention. Sexually Transmitted Disease Surveillance 2014. Atlanta: U.S. Department of Health and Human Services; 2015.

Centers for Disease Control and Prevention. *Sexually Transmitted Disease Surveillance 2014.* Atlanta: U.S. Department of Health and Human Services; 2015. Retrieved from: http://www.cdc.gov/std/stats14/surv-2014-print.pdf

Centers for Disease Control and Prevention (2007). *Suicide trends among youths and young adults aged 10-24 years—United States, 1990-2004.* Retrieved from website: http://www.cdc.gov/mmwr/preview/mmwrhtml/mm5635a2.htm

Centers for Disease Control and Prevention, National Center for HIV/AIDS, Viral Hepatitis, STD, and TB Prevention. (2016) Today's HIV/AIDS epidemic. Accessed June 20, 2016 from http://www.cdc.gov/nchhstp/newsroom/docs/factsheets/todaysepidemic-508.pdf

Centers for Disease Control and Prevention. "Update: AIDS Among Women— United States, 1994." MMWR 44:81-84, 1995.

Centers for Disease Control and Prevention, National Centers for Injury Prevention and Control. Web-based Injury Statistics Query and Reporting System (WISQARS) [online]. (2005) Accessed June 20, 2016 from www.cdc.gov/injury/wisqars

Chandra A, Stephen EH. "Impaired Fecundity in the United States: 1982-1995." *Fam Plan Persp,* 30:34-42, 1998.

Chang J, Elam-Evans LD, Berg CJ, Herndon J, Flowers L, Seed KA, Syverson CJ. (2003) Pregnancy-Related Mortality Surveillance—United States, 1991-1999. Accessed on May 20, 2017 from the Centers for Disease Control Website: https://www.cdc.gov/mmwr/preview/mmwrhtml/ss5202a1.htm

Clarke, S. Centers for Disease Control and Prevention, National Center for Health Statistics. (1995). Monthly vital statistics report: Advance report of final divorce statistics, 1989 and 1990 (Vol. 43, No. 9, Supplement). Retrieved from website on June 15, 2016: http://www.cdc.gov/nchs/data/mvsr/supp/mv43_09s.pdf

Conceptions Reproductive Associates of Colorado. In Vitro Fertilization Costs, Retrieved on June 26, 2018 from http://www.conceptionsrepro.com/ivf-costs.html#package1

Copen, CE. Condom use during sexual intercourse among women and men aged 15-44 in the United States: 2011-2015 National Survey of Family Growth. National health statistics reports; no. 105. Hyattsville, MD: National Center for Health Statistics. 2017.

Creasy RK. "Preterm Labor and Delivery." *Maternal-Fetal Medicine: Principles and Practices.* Creasy RK, Resnik R (Eds). W.B. Saunders Co., Philadelphia, 1984.

Daniels K, Daugherty J, Jones J, Mosher W, Division of Vital Statistics. (2015) Current Contraceptive Use and Variation by Selected Characteristics Among Women Aged 15-44: United States 2011-2013, and Changes in Patterns of Use Since 1995. National Health Statistics Reports Number 60. Center for Disease Control and Prevention, U.S. Department of Health and Human Services. Accessed on June 17, 2016 from CDC website: http://www.cdc.gov/nchs/data/nhsr/nhsr086.pdf

Division of STD Prevention. Sexually Transmitted Disease Surveillance, 1994. U.S. Department of Health and Human Services, Public Health Service. Atlanta: Centers for Disease Control and Prevention, September 1995.

Division of STD Prevention. Sexually Transmitted Disease Surveillance, 1999. Department of Health and Human Services, Atlanta: Centers for Disease Control and Prevention (CDC), September 2000.

Douglas County Health Department. Chlamydia Rates. *Omaha World Herald*. September 2, 2011.

Dusenbery M. "Doing Harm: The Truth About How Bad Medicine and Lazy Science Have Women Dismissed, Misdiagnosed and Sick." First Edition, HarperCollins Publishers, 195 Broadway, New York, New York 10007, 2018.

Ely DM, Hoyert DL. Differences between rural and urban areas in mortality rates for the leading causes of infant death: United States, 2013-2015. NCHS Data Brief, no 300. Hyattsville, MD: National Center for Health Statistics. 2018.

Eng TR, Butler WT, editors; Institute of Medicine (US). Summary: The hidden epidemic: confronting sexually transmitted diseases. Washington (DC): National Academy Press; 1997. p. 43.

Federal Bureau of Investigation, Uniform crime Reports as prepared by the National Archive of Criminal Justice Data. (2012) Estimated crime in United States-Total. Accessed June 20, 2016

Federal Interagency Forum on Child and Family Statistics. "America's Children: Key National Indicators of Well-Being, 2003." Washington DC: US Government Printing Office.

Fehring RJ. (2015) The influence of contraception, abortion, and natural family planning on divorce rates as found in the 2006-2010 National Survey of Family Growth, The Linacre Quarterly, 82(3), 273-282.

Fehring RJ. (2014) The Influence of Ever Use of Natural Family Planning and Contraceptive Methods on Divorce Rates as Found in the 2006-2010 National Survey of Family Growth, The Linacre Quarterly 81(2), 190-194.

Ferraretti AP, Goossens V, Mouzon J, et al. Assisted reproductive technology in Europe, 2008: results generated from European registers by ESHRE. Human Reproduction 27(9): 2571-2584, 2012.

Finer LB, Zolna MR. Unintended pregnancy in the United States: Incidence and disparities, 2006. Contraception. 2011; 84(5): 478-485.

Fitzgibbons RP. Growing up with Gay Parents: What is the Big Deal? Linacre Quarterly (2015) 82:332-336.

Ford K. "Contraceptive Utilization, United States." *Vital and Health Statistics,* series 23, no. 2. DHHS Pub No (PHS) 79, 1978. Public Health Service. Washington Office of Health Research, Statistics and Technology, National Center for Health Statistics, Hyattsville, Maryland, September 1979.

GBD 2013 Pediatrics Collaboration. *JAMA Pediatr.* 2015; 315(9): 859.

Gibbs RS. "Impact of Infectious Diseases on Women's Health." 1776-2026. *Obstet Gynecol,* no. 97, 2001, pp. 1019-1023.

Gigant K. "Your Tax Dollars at Work for Planned Parenthood." *Celebrate Life,* 25:42-45, 2003.

Goodwin PY, Mosher WD, Chandra A. Marriage and cohabitation in the United States: A statistical portrait based on Cycle 6 (2002) of the National Survey of Family Growth. National Center for Health Statistics. Vital Health Stat 23(28). 2010.

www.google.com/metaphysics, 2017.

Grimes DA, Wallach M. "Modern Contraception: Updates from the Contraception Report." Emron, Totowa, NJ, 1997.

Hamilton BE, Martin JA, Osterman MJ, Curtin SC, Mathews TJ, Division of Vital Statistics. (2015) Births: Final Data for 2014. National Vital Statistics Reports. Center for Disease Control and Prevention. 64(12). Accessed June 17, 2016 from http://www.cdc.gov/nchs/data/nvsr/nvsr64/nvsr64_12.pdf

Hamilton BE, Mathews TJ. Continued declines in teen births in the United states, 2015. NCHS data brief, no 259. Hyattsville, MD: National Center for Health Statistics. 2016.

Hamilton BE, Rossen LM, Branum AM. Teen birth rates for urban and rural areas in the United States, 2007-2015. NCHS data brief, no 264. Hyattsville, MD: National Center for Health Statistics. 2016.

Hedegaard H, Warner M, Miniño AM. Drug overdose deaths in the United States, 1999-2016. NCHS Data Brief, no 294. Hyattsville, MD: National Center for Health Statistics. 2017.

Hilgers TW. The Medical & Surgical Practice of NaProTECHNOLOGY®. Pope Paul VI Institute Press, Omaha, NE, 2004 (1,244 pages)

Hilgers TW, O'Hare D. "Abortion-related Maternal Mortality: An In-Depth Analysis." *Hilgers TW, Horan DJ, Mall D (Eds). "New Perspectives on Human Abortion."* Aletheia Books, University Publications of America, 1981.

Hunter D. "Outrage, Inc.: How the Liberal Mob Ruined Science, Journalism and Hollywood." HarperCollins Publishers, 195 Broadway, New York, New York, 10007, 2018.

"Infant Mortality and Low Birth Weight Among Black and White Infants — United States, 1980-2000." *Morbidity and Mortality Weekly Report,* 51 (27): 589-592, July 12, 2002.

Infertility Answers. International IVF Costs. Retrieved on June 26, 2018 from http://infertilityanswers.org/international_ivf_costs

Jones J, Mosher W, Daniels K, Division of Vital Statistics. (2012) Current Contraceptive Use in the United States 2006-2010, and Changes in Patterns of Use Since 1995. National Health Statistics Reports Number 60. Center for Disease Control and Prevention, U.S. Department of Health and Human Services. Accessed on June 17, 2016 from CDC website: http://www.cdc.gov/nchs/data/nhsr/nhsr060.pdf

Keslar L.: The Rise of Fake Medical News. In: Proto, Massachusetts General Hospital/Dispatches from the Frontiers of Medicine. Summer Edition, 2018.

Kluger B. So long Hef, thanks for the gig. *USA Today,* 29 Sept. 2017, p. 7A

Kochanek KD, Murphy SL, Xu JQ, Arias E. Mortality in the United States, 2016. NCHS Data Brief, no 293. Hyattsville, MD: National Center for Health Statistics. 2017.

The Linacre Quarterly: Journal of the Catholic Medical Association Vol. 84, No. 1, 2017.

Linderman J, Fenn L, Horn B, Pana E. "Teens Growing Up Under Fire." USA Today/Associated Press Investigations, In: USA Today Weekend, September 8-10, 2017, p. 1A.

The Los Angeles Times. 'Sea of despair' behind increase in death rates among whites. Omaha World Herald, March 25, 2017.

MacDorman MF, Gregory ECW. Fetal and perinatal mortality: United States, 2013. National vital statistics reports; vol 64 no 8. Hyattsville, MD: National Center for Health Statistics. 2015.

Martin JA, Hamilton BE, Osterman MJK. Births in the United States, 2014. NCHS data brief, no 216. Hyattsville, MD: National Center for Health Statistics. 2015.

Martin JA, Hamilton BE, Ventura SJ, et al. "Births: Final Data for 2000." *National Center for Health Statistics,* vol. 50, no. 5, 2002.

Martin JA, Kirmeyer S, Osterman M, Shepherd RA. Born a bit too early: Recent trends in late preterm births. NCHS data brief, no 24. Hyattsville, MD: National Center for Health Statistics. 2009.

Martin JA, Park MM. "Trends in Twin and Triplet Births: 1980-1997." *National Vital Statistics Report,* vol. 47, no. 24, National Center for Health Statistics, Hyattsville, Maryland, 1999.

Mathews TJ, Ely DM, Driscoll AK. State variations in infant mortality by race and Hispanic origin of mother, 2013-2015. NCHS Data Brief, no 295. Hyattsville, MD: National Center for Health Statistics. 2018.

McManus MJ. (2011) Confronting the More Entrenched Foe: The Disaster of No-Fault Divorce and Its Legacy of Cohabitation. The Family in America. 25(2). 157-172.

MD Anderson Cancer Center. www.mcanderson.org (Cancer—types, March 5, 2017).

Menacker F, Hamilton BE. Recent trends in cesarean delivery in the United States. NCHS data brief, no 35. Hyattsville, MD: National Center for Health Statistics. 2010.

Michael RT. "Why did the U.S. Divorce Rate Double Within a Decade?" *Research in Population Economics,* no. 6, 1988, pp. 367-399.

Mørch LS, Skovlund CW, Hannaford PC, Iversen L, Fielding S, Lidegaard Ø. Contemporary Hormonal Contraception and the Risk of Breast Cancer. The New England Journal of Medicine 377(23): 2228-2277, 2017.

Moreno V, Bosch X, Munoz N, et al. "Effect of Oral Contraceptives on Risk of Cervical Cancer in Women with Human Papilloma Virus Infection: The IARC Multicentric Case-Control Study." *Lancet,* 359:1085-1092, 2002.

Mosher SW. "The Uncontrolled AIDS Epidemic." *Population Research Institute Review,* 13:3, 2003.

Mosher WD, (1982) Trends in Contraceptive Practice, United States, 1965-76. National Center for Health Statistics. Vital and Health Statistics 23 (10). Accessed on June 17, 2016 from CDC Website: http://www.cdc.gov/nchs/data/series/sr_23/sr23_010.pdf

Mosher WD, Bacharach CA. "Contraceptive Use: United States, 1980." *Vital and Health Statistics,* series 23, no. 12. DHHS Pub No (PHS) 86, 1988.

Mosher WD, Bachrach CA. Contraceptive Use United States, 1982. Vital and Health Statistics Series 23 No. 12. National Center for Health Statistics. Accessed on June 17, 2016 from CDC website: http://www.cdc.gov/nchs/data/series/sr_23/sr23_012.pdf

Mosher WD, Jones J. (2010) Use of contraception in the United States: 1982-2008. National Center for Health Statistics. Vital and Health Statistics 23(29). Accessed on June 17, 2016 from CDC Website: http://www.cdc.gov/nchs/data/series/sr_23/sr23_029.pdf

Mosher WD, Pratt WF. "Contraceptive Use in the United States: 1982-1990." *Advanced Data from Vital and Health Statistics,* no. 182, 1990. Hyattsville, Maryland: National Center for Health Statistics, Washington DC.

National Center for Chronic Disease Prevention and Health Promotion, Division of Reproductive Health, Assisted Reproductive Technology National Summary Report, 2010.

National Center for Chronic Disease Prevention and Health Promotion, Division of Reproductive Health, Assisted Reproductive Technology National Summary Report, 2013.

National Center for Chronic Disease Prevention and Health Promotion, Division of Reproductive Health, Assisted Reproductive Technology National Summary Report, 2015.

National Center for Chronic Disease Prevention and Health Promotion, Division of Reproductive Health, Assisted Reproductive Technology National Summary Report, 2014.

National Center for Health Statistics. (1991) Annual Summary of Births, Marriages, Divorces, and Deaths: United States, 1990. Monthly Vital Statistics Report. 39(13) Retrieved from CDC website on June 15, 2016: http://www.cdc.gov/nchs/data/mvsr/supp/mv39_13.pdf

National Center for Health Statistics. (1992) Annual Summary of Births, Marriages, Divorces, and Deaths: United States, 1991. Monthly Vital Statistics Report. 40(13) Retrieved from CDC website on June 15, 2016: http://www.cdc.gov/nchs/data/mvsr/supp/mv40_13.pdf

National Center for Health Statistics. (1993) Annual Summary of Births, Marriages, Divorces, and Deaths: United States, 1992. Monthly Vital Statistics Report. 41(13) Retrieved from CDC website on June 15, 2016: http://www.cdc.gov/nchs/data/mvsr/supp/mv41_13.pdf

National Center for Health Statistics. (1994) Annual Summary of Births, Marriages, Divorces, and Deaths: United States, 1993. Monthly Vital Statistics Report. 42(13) Retrieved from CDC website on June 15, 2016: http://www.cdc.gov/nchs/data/mvsr/supp/mv42_13acc.pdf

National Center for Health Statistics. (1995) Annual Summary of Births, Marriages, Divorces, and Deaths: United States, 1994. Monthly Vital Statistics Report. 43(13) Retrieved from CDC website on June 15, 2016: http://www.cdc.gov/nchs/data/mvsr/mv43_13.pdf

National Center for Health Statistics. (1996) Annual Summary of Births, Marriages, Divorces, and Deaths for 1995. Monthly Vital Statistics Report. 44(12) Retrieved from CDC website on June 15, 2016: http://www.cdc.gov/nchs/data/mvsr/mv44_12.pdf

National Center for Health Statistics. (1997) Annual Summary of Births, Marriages, Divorces, and Deaths for 1996. Monthly Vital Statistics Report. 45(12) Retrieved from CDC website on June 15, 2016: http://www.cdc.gov/nchs/data/mvsr/mv45_12.pdf

National Center for Health Statistics. (1998) Annual Summary of Births, Marriages, Divorces, and Deaths for 1997. Monthly Vital Statistics Report. 46(12) Retrieved from CDC website on June 15, 2016: http://www.cdc.gov/nchs/data/mvsr/mv46_12.pdf

National Center for Health Statistics, Center for Disease Control and Prevention. (1999) Births, Marriages, Divorces, Provisional Data for 1998. National Vital Statistics Reports. 47(21). Retrieved from CDC website on June 15, 2016: http://www.cdc.gov/nchs/data/nvsr/nvsr47/nvs47_21.pdf

National Center for Health Statistics, Center for Disease Control and Prevention. (2001) Births, Marriages, Divorces, Provisional Data for 1999. National Vital Statistics Reports. 48(19). Retrieved from CDC website on June 15, 2016: http://www.cdc.gov/nchs/data/nvsr/nvsr48/nvs48_19.pdf

National Legal center for the Medically Dependent and Disabled, Inc. (2014) Issues in Law and Medicine, Vol 29, No. 2.

National Longitudinal Survey of Adolescent Health, Wave II, 1996. Cited in: A Report of the Heritage Center for Data Analysis. Recker RE, Johnson KA, Noyes LR: Sexually Active Teenagers are Most Likely to be Depressed and to Attempt Suicide. The Heritage

National Center for Vital Statistics Report, vol. 50, no. 5, Feb. 12, 2002.

NCADV (2015), www.NCADV.org.

Nina Desai. The Road to Single Embryo Transfers in IVF. Ob/Gyn & Women's Health Institute 2017 Year in Review, Cleveland Clinic, 2017.

Nygren K, Finnström O, Källén B, Olausson PO. Population-based Swedish studies of outcomes after *in vitro* fertilization. Acta Obstetricia et Gynecologica 86: 774-782, 2007.

O'Carroll P, Mercy J, Hersey J, Casey B, Odell-Butler M. Centers for Disease Control, National Center for Injury Prevention and Control, U.S. Department of Health and Human Services, Public Health Service. (1992) *Youth suicide prevention programs: A resource guide.* Retrieved from website: http:// wonder.cdc.gov/wonder/prevguid/p0000024/p0000024.asp

O'Donnell J, Saker A. 'What ifs' plague parents of teen suicides. *USA Today,* 20 March 2018, p. 3A.

O'Dowd MJ, Philipp EE. "The History of Obstetrics and Gynecology." *Parthenon Publishing Group,* New York, 1994.

Oqunwak AN, Anderson MC, Sangi—Haghpeykar H: IPV During Pregnancy...J Repro Med. 62: 65-71, 2017.

Osterman MJK, Martin JA. Trends in low-risk cesarean delivery in the United States, 1990-2013. National vital statistics reports; vol 63 no 6. Hyattsville, MD: National Center for Health Statistics. 2014.

Painter K. U.S. life expectancy drops for second year. *USA Today,* 21 Dec. 2017, p. 3A.

Parker S. The collapse of marriage across the board. *Midlands Business Journal,* 22 Sept. 2017, p. 13

Pazol K, Creanga AA, Jamieson DJ. (2015) Abortion Surveillance—United States, 2012. Accessed on May 20, 2017 from the Centers for Disease Control and Prevention Website: https://www.cdc.gov/mmwr/preview/mmwrhtml/ ss6410a1.htm?s_cid=ss6410a1_w

Peterson LS. "Contraceptive Use in the United States: 1982-1990." *Advanced Data from Vital and Health Statistics,* no. 260, 1995. Hyattsville, Maryland: National Center for Health Statistics, Washington DC.

Peterson LS, Division of Vital Statistics. (1995) Contraceptive Use in the United States: 1982-90. Advance Data No. 260. Vital and Health Statistics, Centers for Disease Control and Prevention, National Center for Health Statistics. Retrieved from the CDC Website on June 17, 2016: http:// www.cdc.gov/nchs/data/ad/ad260.pdf

Rector RE, Johnson KA, Noyes LR. "Report: Sexually Active Teenagers are More Likely to be Depressed and to Attempt Suicide. A Report of a Heritage Center for Data Analysis." Washington, DC, 2003.

Resolve. The Costs of Infertility Treatment, Accessed from http://www.resolve. org/family-building-options/insurance_coverage/the-costs-of-infertility-treatment.html

SAMHASA Office of Applied Studies. "National Household Survey on Drug Abuse," 1999.

Schlesselman JJ. "Cancer of the Breast and Reproductive Tract in Relation to Use of Oral Contraceptives." *Contraception,* 40:1-38, 1989.

Schlesselman JJ. "Net Effect of Oral Contraceptive Use on the Risk of Cancer in Women in the United States." *Obstet Gynecol,* 85:793-801, 1995.

Schlesselman JJ. "Oral Contraceptives in Breast Cancer." *Am J Obstet Gynecol,* 163:1379-1387, 1990.

Sells CW, Blum RW. "Morbidity and Mortality Among U.S. Adolescents: An Overview of Data and Trends." *AM J Pub Health,* 86:513-519, 1996.

"Sexually-Transmitted Disease Surveillance, 1994." *Division of STD/HIV Prevention, U.S. Department of Health and Human Services, Public Health Service.* Atlanta: Center for Disease Control, September 1995.

Skovlund CW, Morch LS, Kessing LV, Lidegaard: Association of Hormonal Contraception with Depression. JAMA Psychiatry 73(11):1154-62, 2016.

Social Trends Institute. "The Cohabitation-Go-Round: Cohabitation and Family Instability Across the Globe." *World Family Map,* 2017.

Sourcebook of criminal justice statistics online. Retrieved on June 26, 2018 from https://www.albany.edu/sourcebook//pdf/t4262009.pdf

Statistical Abstract of the United States, 1981 edition, Table 49; 1986 edition, Table 45; 1990 edition, Table 49; 1993 edition, Table 61; 1998 edition, Table 64; 2002 edition, Table 48; 2006 edition, Table 51; and 2010 edition, Table 57.

Statistical Abstract of the United States, 1982-83 edition, Table 124, for years 1960 and 1965; 2001 edition, Table 116, for years 1970 to 1995. For later years, provisional data from *National Vital Statistics Reports,* 49.6 (August 22, 2001), 54.20 (July 21, 2006), and 58.25 (August 27, 2010).

STD Surveillance Summary 2014

Sunderam S, Kissin DM, Crawford SB, Folger SG, Jamieson DJ, Warner L, Barfield WD. (2015) Assisted Reproductive Technology Surveillance—United States, 2013. Accessed on May 20, 2017 from the Centers for Disease Control and Prevention Website: https://www.cdc.gov/mmwr/preview/mmwrhtml/ss6411a1.htm?s_cid=ss6411a1_w

Syska BJ, Hilgers TW, O'Hare D. "An Objective Model for Estimating Criminal Abortions and its Implications for Public Policy." *Hilgers TW, Horan DJ, Mall D (Eds). "New Perspectives on Human Abortion."* Aletheia Books, University Publications of America, 1981.

Thomas DB. "Oral Contraceptives and Breast Cancer: Review of the Epidemiological Literature." *Oral Contraceptives and Breast Cancer.* Committee on the Relationship Between Oral-Contraceptives and Breast Cancer. Institute of Medicine, Division of Health Promotion and Disease Prevention. Washington, DC: National Academy Press; 1991.

"Trends in "Prematurity" United States: 1950-1967." *National Center for Health Statistics, U.S. Department of HEW*, Publication No. (HSM) 72-1030, Rockville, Maryland, January 1972. No. 15, Series 3.

U.S. Census Bureau, Current Population Survey, Annual Social and Economic Supplement, 1967 to present. Table AD3. Living arrangements of adults 35 to 64 years old, 1967 to present. Retrieved July 18, 2016 from http://www.census.gov/hhes/families/data/adults.html

U.S. Census Bureau, Current Population Survey, Annual Social and Economic Supplement, 1967 to present. Table AD3. Living arrangements of adults 25 to 34 years old, 1967 to present. Retrieved July 18, 2016 from http://www.census.gov/hhes/families/data/adults.html

U.S. Census Bureau, Current Population Survey, Annual Social and Economic Supplement, 1967 to present. Table AD3. Living arrangements of adults 18 to 24 years old, 1967 to present. Retrieved July 18, 2016 from http://www.census.gov/hhes/families/data/adults.html

U.S. Census Bureau, Current Population Survey, Annual Social and Economic Supplements 1967 to Present. Table AD-2. Living Arrangements of Adults 18 and Over, 1967 to Present. (2015) Accessed June 16, 2016. Retrieved from the U.S. Census Bureau Website: http://www.census.gov/hhes/families/data/adults.html

U.S. Census Bureau, Current Population Survey, Annual Social and Economic Supplement, 1967-2015. Figure AD-3a. Living arrangements of adults 18 and over. Retrieved from Census Bureau Website: http://www.census.gov

U.S. Census Bureau Data for 1975-1997. Statistical Abstract of the United States (121st Edition), Washington DC, 2001.

U.S. Census Bureau, Decennial Census, 1960, and Current Population Survey, Annual Social and Economic Supplements 1968 to 2015. Ch-1 Living Arrangements of Children Under 18 Years Old; 1960 to Present. (2015) Accessed June 16, 2016. Retrieved from the U.S. Census Bureau Website: http://www.census.gov/hhes/families/data/children.html

U.S. Census Bureau, Decennial Census, 1960, and Current Population Survey, Annual Social and Economic Supplements 1968 to 2015. Ch-5 Children Under 18 Years Living with Mother Only, buy Marital Status of Mother: 1960 to 2014. (2015) Accessed June 16, 2016. Retrieved from the U.S. Census Bureau Website: http://www.census.gov/hhes/families/data/children.html

U.S. Census Bureau, Decennial Census, 1960, and Current Population Survey, Annual Social and Economic Supplements, 1968 to 2015. Figure CH-1. Living arrangements of children: 1960 to present. Retrieved from Census Bureau Website: http://www.census.gov

U.S. Census Bureau, Population Division (2011). Table 1. Intercensal Estimates of Resident Population by Sex and Age for the United States: April 1, 2000 to July 1, 2010. National Intercensal Estimates (2000-2012). Retrieved from the U.S. Census Bureau Website on June 15, 2016: http://www.census.gov/popest/data/intercensal/national/nat2010.html

U.S. Census Bureau, Population Division, American Fact Finder (2014). Monthly Population Estimates for the United States: April 1, 2012 to December 1, 2014. Retrieved from American Fact Finder Website on June 15, 2016: http://factfinder.census.gov/faces/tableservices/jsf/pages/productview.xhtml?src=bkmk

U.S. Census Bureau, Population division. (2004) Resident Population plus Armed Forces Overseas—Estimates by Age, Sex, and Race: July 1, 1965. Accessed June 17, 2016 from Census Bureau Website: https://www.census.gov/popest/data/national/asrh/pre-1980/PE-11.html

U.S. Census Bureau, Population division. (2004) Resident Population plus Armed Forces Overseas—Estimates by Age, Sex, and Race: July 1, 1973. Accessed June 17, 2016 from Census Bureau Website: https://www.census.gov/popest/data/national/asrh/pre-1980/PE-11.html

U.S. Census Bureau, Population division. (2004) Resident Population plus Armed Forces Overseas—Estimates by Age, Sex, and Race: July 1, 1976. Accessed June 17, 2016 from Census Bureau Website: https://www.census.gov/popest/data/national/asrh/pre-1980/PE-11.html

U.S. Census Bureau, Population division. (2004) Resident Population Estimates of the United States by Age and Sex: April 1, 1990 to July 1, 1999, with Short-Term Projection to November 1, 2000. Accessed June 17, 2016 from Census Bureau Website: https://www.census.gov/popest/data/historical/1990s/index.html

Ventura SJ, Bachrach CA. "Non-Marital Childbearing in the United State, 1940-1999." *National Vital Statistics Reports. Center for Disease Control and Prevention,* 48:1-40, October 18, 2000.

Ventura SJ, Bachrach CA, Division of Vital Statistics, National Center for Health Statistics, National Institute of Child Health and Human Development. (2000) Nonmarital Childbearing in the United States, 1940-99 (Revised). National Vital Statistics Reports. Center for Disease Control and Prevention. 48(16). Accessed June 17, 2016 from https://www.cdc.gov/nchs/data/nvsr/nvsr48/nvs48_16.pdf

Ventura SJ, Curtin SC, Abma JC, Henshaw SK. Estimated pregnancy rates and rates of pregnancy outcomes for the United States, 1990-2008. National vital statistics reports; vol 60 no 7. Hyattsville, MD: National Center for Health Statistics. 2012.

Ventura SJ, Mosher WD, Henshaw S. "Revised Pregnancy Rates, 1990-1997 and New Rates for 1998-1999." *National Vital Statistics Reports, Center for Disease Control and Prevention,* 52:1-16, October 31, 2003.

Vital and Health Statistics. National Center for Health Statistics. "Triplet Births: Trends and Outcomes, 1971-1994." January 1997.

Vital and Health Statistics. "Supplements to the Monthly Vital Statistics Report." Series 24, no. 9, 2003.

Wang YA, Sullivan EA, Black D, et al. Preterm birth and low birth weight after assisted reproductive technology-related pregnancy in Australia between 1996 and 2000. Fertility and Sterility 83(6): 1650-1658, 2005.

Washington Post. Gonorrhea Risks 'Becoming an Untreatable Disease.' December 2015, Accessed 22 May 2017.

Webster's II New College Dictionary. Houghton Mifflin Co., Boston, 2001

Weed S. " Research Update on Promoting Chastity Among adolescents." 16th Annual Meeting, *American Academy of Fertility Care Professionals,* July 18, 1997.

Wisborg K, Ingerslev HJ, Henriksen TB. In vitro fertilization and preterm delivery, low birth weight, and admission to the neonatal intensive care unit: a prospective follow-up study. Fertility and Sterility 94(6): 2102-2106, 2010.

Woodring J, Kruszon-Moran D, McQuillan G. HIV infection in U.S. household population aged 18-59: Data from National Health and Nutrition Examination Survey, 2007-2012. National health statistics reports; no 83. Hyattsville, MD: National Center for Health Statistics. 2015.

Womack LS, Rossen LM, Martin JA. Singleton low birthweight rates, by race and Hispanic origin: United States, 2006-2016. NCHS Data Brief, no 306. Hyattsville, MD: National Center for Health Statistics. 2018.

Wu AK, Elliott P, Katz PP, Smith JF. "Time costs of fertility care: the hidden hardship of building a family." *Fertill Steril* 99(7):2025-30, 2013.

Wu, AK. et al. "Out-of-pocket fertility patient expense: data from a multicenter prospective infertility cohort." *The Journal of urology* 191(2):427-32, 2014.

Zablotsky B, Black LI, Blumberg SJ. Estimated prevalence of children with diagnosed developmental disabilities in the United States, 2014-2016. NCHS Data Brief, no 291. Hyattsville, MD: National Center for Health Statistics. 2017.

Zethraeus N, Dreber A, Ranehill E, et al. A first-choice combined oral contraceptive influences general well-being in healthy women: a double-blind, randomized, placebo-controlled trial. Fertility and Sterility 107(5): 1238-1245, 2017.

Index